Leadership

It Ain't Rocket Science!

A Critical Analysis of Moving with the Cheese
and Other Motivational Leadership
BULLSHIT

I0494844

Dedication:

To my mother Sylvia for "effektivitet och arbetsglädje."
You know what I mean.

TABLE OF CONTENTS

WHAT IS LEADERSHIP?

"To see what is right and not to do it is cowardice."
— Confucius, Chinese philosopher (551-479 BCE)

The evening was nearing its end. In a few hours the alarm clock would wake me from sweet dreams of snow and sun and sky. Then the struggle would begin. I would fight my way through the morning rush hour traffic only to fall asleep an hour later in the leadership seminar I would be attending, although that might be a good thing. Someone had called me a "loose cannon" once. I knew when it was better to hold my horses than speak the truth. Tomorrow would be black Monday morning.

"Tomorrow will be black *diamond* morning," insisted Bubba, my police officer friend who is also a skier. "You will be living on the memory of the ski hills, on the challenge of that final run down the black diamond slope."

I thought about the upcoming seminar. They call it leadership and I hate it because it smacks of human nature, yet nobody sees the forest for the trees. Was I being trite? I turned and looked out the window. The mountain was calling my name. Oh, let me throw off this cape that is suffocating me, let me trade my old lance for one with a sharper edge. I was thinking metaphorically, of course. Morning rush hour . . . I looked at Bubba across the table.

"Black *diamond* morning? You've got to be kidding!"

The cookbook approach to leadership . . . a simple recipe for success . . . Yeah, all you need is a positive attitude and the stop-lights will magically change to go-lights . . . This is the essence of what is wrong with modern leadership studies.

"This coworker of mine crashed his truck into a building and made a hole large enough to walk through," I said. "Management placed him on probationary status, which the rest of us thought a bit lenient considering the nature of his offense. But what really hit us was when the guy was promoted to supervisor six months later. The fact that he crashed the truck and destroyed the building, and perhaps even jeopardized our safety, did not bother us nearly as much as what management did, or *failed* to do, about the fact that he crashed the truck, destroyed the building, and jeopardized our safety."

"At my job," Bubba said, "police officers sometimes nap in their cars while their buddies stand watch, even though it is against company policy."

"How do you deal with it?" I asked. Bubba had been promoted to sergeant just last year. "How do you deal with your team breaking the rules, the same rules you would have broken just days before your promotion?"

I might have been looking for an argument, but Bubba was my friend and I was confident I could talk to him. If he had an answer, he would tell me. If he were wrong, he would admit it.

"I tell them that my position prevents me from turning my head," he said. He paused and searched for a way to justify his answer. "When a cop is tired, he is welcome to nap in my office for half an hour while I cover for him."

"But why was it okay for you and your buddies to sleep in your cars prior to your promotion but not after your promotion?" I asked. "The only thing that has changed is your title."

I recalled an incidence a few years ago when I had caught my supervisor breaking a rule he had been preaching to us about for years. "Hah! I just caught you!" I said, feeling smug. But he just smiled and explained that he was not really breaking the rule; he was just *bending* it to facilitate efficiency. In briefing later he concluded, "You do what you want as long as it's safe. Just don't let me catch you!"

"Here is the gist of my problem," I said to Bubba. "I have been following the rules for twenty years, while my coworkers and supervisors have been breaking the rules for twenty years. Granted, some of these rules deserve to be broken, but that is a different story. My question is, why are the supervisors still supervisors, why are my coworkers not punished, and why am I not rewarded?"

Bubba smiled. "Simple! You are not seeing the big picture. The leadership is, in fact, punishing you, the good worker, for following the rules, and rewarding your coworkers for breaking them. You've got to know how to play the game."

But to what avail? The down-turned economy since 9/11 has caused tens of thousands of people to lose their jobs. At my company numerous supervisors have been demoted to grunts. Just last month I observed a former supervisor mistreating customer property. Had he observed me doing the same while he was still wearing the patch, he would no doubt have disciplined me, given me time off without pay, maybe even become the instrument of my termination.

"Some of our leaders pick up overtime as grunts," I said. "When they are leaders they stress the rules, but when they work as grunts, which may be just hours later in the same day, the rules suddenly become less important."

"Kind of like a cop who is speeding or doesn't wear his seatbelt when off duty," Bubba suggested.

Was he being facetious? I pointed my finger at him. "Kind of like *you*, who don't wear your helmet when riding your motorcycle during off-hours. Leadership is not a nine-to-five job; it's a lifestyle!"

I related to Bubba how disappointed I was when I told my supervisor that I could see our company from my kitchen window, and he answered, "Who wants to look at *that* on their day off? I would lower the blinds!" The moment he stripped out of his uniform he was no longer a leader. He did, in fact, see leadership as a nine-to-five job.

Bubba took a sip of his coffee. "What criteria determine a good leader?"

I shrugged. "The most important may be the use of common sense."

"And there is, of course, the issue of integrity and respect," said Bubba. "There should be no doubt how the leader feels about the team and his position as a leader. If you were left with the task of choosing the best leader for your company, team, group, or regiment, what qualities would you look for and why?"

"He must be loyal and fair to those who trust him," I said, but then caught myself. "Is that not obvious? Are we not just rehashing the same ideas and slogans people have been mouthing for centuries? What constitutes loyal and fair? What are the deeper meanings of those words? Give some examples."

"You develop a gut feeling for what makes your team tick," Bubba suggested.

I waved it off. "Good idea, but too vague. And how do you punish or reprimand when it is called for? Would not failing to do so place your integrity on the line?"

"Excessive sternness or self-serving interests result in dictatorship," said Bubba.

"Yeah, but where do you draw the line? What type of leader does it take to survive the scrutiny of his team?"

We sat in silence. People say they wish to be leaders because they think they can make a difference. But how? A difference to the company? A difference to themselves? A difference to those they lead? The followers, including the leader's antagonists and critics, may be his best source of information when determining how successful he is making a difference.

"Does the leader have a serious interest in being a good leader?" Bubba asked. "The obvious answer is *yes*, of course, but how does he know? From where does his motivation stem? Can he name one specific and truthful reason for desiring to be a leader; that is, without mentioning the higher salary of his position or the elevation in status to his name?"

"The leader's gut feeling must be balanced by logic and intellect, curiosity and maturity, open-mindedness and self-reflection," I said.

"It might also be in place to mention the value of the Golden Rule," said Bubba, "which is probably the only rule that has truly stood the test of time."

Hah! I clenched my fists and smiled. The Golden Rule . . . what a beautiful ring in our ears. But it is much too simplistic when the problems start building right in front of our noses. My thoughts turned to the famous quote attributed to former American President Harry S. Truman: *It is amazing what you can accomplish, if you don't care who gets the credit.* I glanced at Bubba and wanted to ask: What were the times and circumstances when Truman uttered those words? What were the personalities of the people involved? What were their backgrounds, goals, and desires? How can you remove an idea from a time sixty years in the past, and with the swift lash of your tongue transport it to the immediacy of today and place it in a different group of people, under a different set of circumstances; in short, in a different world, and think that nothing has changed?

Winning matters. And it matters who gets the credit, and I knew why. I will take winning over losing any day. Contrary to popular belief, it is not a matter of how you play the game. No, you must win to acquire a following. But the leader's job is not to win at all cost. Nobody on the team will sacrifice his or her family or health just for the leader. Nor is the leader's repute determined solely by the job he performs or by the company for which he works. You can be a supervisor, a boss, or a dictator; you can inspire fear, threaten, coerce, and blackmail; you can sweet talk and bribe; but you can lead only if you have a following. Think about this: In his heyday even Adolf Hitler was one hell of a role model.

"Being a good leader is not the best job in the world; working for one is," Bubba said.

And I agreed, most definitely, but we still had not clarified anything beyond the obvious, and the issue raised yet another problem: What if you are leading your people toward disaster and don't even know it? I imagined a bunch of workers walking in a circle. *The person at the head of the line must know where we are going*, says one of them. Yeah, right!

I told Bubba how my company has six employees on suspension right now. One of them got suspended for cussing at the supervisor. Although this may be a legitimate reason for suspension, those who know the supervisor also know that his own language is far from clean. In fact, you may be standing right in his office when he leans over on one butt cheek and farts in your direction, with no apology coming your way.

"The leader is part of the elite; that is why he is a leader," Bubba said. "The leader understands the company, its tradition, values, and goals."

"I know the good leaders at my job," I said. "I know them without knowing them well. If I have a problem, I say to myself: Where do I go for help? And the right leader automatically pops up in my mind. Leadership requires knowledge and organizational skill, but it requires something more. It requires character.

Character means integrity, and it is the one quality that gains you the support of your team."

"Fighting passionately for a cause is more important than having no cause for which to fight," Bubba said.

"Fighting passionately for a cause is important even if the cause for which you fight is disagreeable to the team," I said.

"It is better with an honest foe than an inconsistent friend," Bubba said. "At least you know what you've got."

And I agreed. The team will detect insincerity. If you bluff now, it will be impossible to command respect later. But being simple is not simple. Not knowing where you stand is simple. Being complicated is simple. Being complicated is being deceptive. The team does not like to be deceived. The team knows if you are a wimp or a warrior. The purpose of leadership is not to improve the leader in the form of ego, money, convenience, or job security.

"Spotting a leader by his or her looks is difficult. Spotting a leader by his or her demeanor is easy," I said. "You know when a leader walks into the room, because he fills the space and you can feel it."

"Are good leaders born or made?" Bubba asked.

It was the age-old question of nature or nurture. Although the world's greatest leaders comprise both genders, all ages and physical builds, and come from a variety of countries and backgrounds, they don't necessarily have anything in common— other than an ability to lead.

"I believe good leaders are born." I said.

"I don't," said Bubba. He looked smug. "They are made. They are most definitely made."

"You're wrong," I said. "The leader gains the support of his team because he knows how to make the team tick. He is born with this sixth sense of human behavior."

"Human behavior can be changed."

I shrugged. "Perhaps, but only at a considerable cost. Try a risk/benefit analysis sometime, and you will likely find that the price for change far outweighs its value. A good leader understands human nature and avoids going against the grain. Although he indicates that the goals are achievable, he is not gung-ho. Most people are not interested in changing who they are or willing to wander too far from their comfort zone."

"Sometimes they have to change for the good of the corporation," Bubba said.

"Yes, but good leaders question, experiment, and research before asking their team to change. They have vision and can look beyond the moment."

"The goal of the team is not to serve itself . . . or is it?" Bubba paused and looked at me. "You know, I think we might be wasting our time with this discussion."

I thought he might be right, but I was not ready to let go. "Maybe wasting time isn't so bad?"

"I think it is," said Bubba. "Don't waste it. Work smarter and not harder."

"There is a difference between working hard and being productive," I said. "And sometimes it is better to go into hiding. Sometimes you have to know when to step forward and when to step back."

"Telling somebody what to do is easy; telling them how to do it is difficult," Bubba offered. "Stating the facts is easy; adding insight is difficult. Pointing out what is wrong is easy; showing how to fix it is difficult. At least it is a challenge if you want to avoid imposing your subjective beliefs on your team."

"So now leadership is subjective?"

"It's raining," said Bubba.

I looked out the window. It wasn't raining, nor snowing. The sun was shining from a blazing blue sky, and the hills were still calling my name.

"But if it were raining," Bubba said, "would it be good or bad?"

"I suppose it depends on whether or not you want to go down the black diamond slope one more time," I said.

"Bingo!"

Is the glass half-full or half-empty? It depends on what we wish to achieve. Your personality traits don't determine your leadership skills, but rather what you do with these traits, and your timing. Whether you are patient or impatient, outspoken or quiet, opinionated or flexible, energetic or laid back has little meaning unless these traits are placed within the context of what the situation demands. A leader who is unable to maintain calm under pressure is neither good nor bad, until we have evaluated the circumstances under which the pressure is applied and the results of his response. Yet we often decide what sounds good beforehand. Although a leader should have good communication skills, is he necessarily ineffective if he is of a quiet nature? My manager once told me that I should not be afraid to speak up and tell my team what I expect of them. I felt like I had just been run over by a steamroller. I had worked for him for nearly ten years, and he knew absolutely nothing about me! My point is that my team loved working with me and did what needed to be done without me bossing them around.

"We need leaders because somebody must tell us how far we have come," I said. "Moving forward without a leader is like writing a book by copying the words of others."

"The best leaders draw from the resourcefulness of their team and take the team beyond the leader's own level of skill," Bubba said. "The best leaders are respected for their courage and honesty even when they are carriers of bad news. Beyond defining the steps, good leadership requires the ability to read between the lines, to see what is *not* there. Leadership is more about *how* to travel the road than which road to take."

* * * * *

My need to write this book has sprung from a life-long desire to be part of a successful, tough, and ambitious team; the type of team an outsider would envy. But this book is not about Bubba and me. If truth be told, I don't even like leadership books that start with parables. However, parables employing the question/answer/discussion approach prove popular for engaging the reader, and have been used successfully to drive home a point even hundreds of years ago. Consider for instance *The Art of War*, the famous text by Renaissance Florentine statesman Niccolo Machiavelli (1469-1527 CE). In a staged dialogue between Fabrizio Colonna, who was part of the noble and powerful Colonna family in Italy, and the host Cosimo Ruccelai,

Machiavelli stresses the importance of the classical view on warfare through a discussion about the difference between the professional and citizen soldier: "Kings ought, therefore, if they want to live securely, have their infantry composed of men, who, when it is necessary for him to wage war, will willingly go forth to it for love of him, and afterwards when peace comes, more willingly return to their homes," says Fabrizio Colonna. "Truly, this reasoning of yours appears to me well considered," answers Cosimo Ruccelai, "none the less, as it is almost contrary to what I have thought up to now, my mind is not yet purged of every doubt."[1] And so the discussion goes forth until every detail is pounded out and hopefully clearly understood by the reader. *Leadership and Self-Deception: Getting Out of the Box*, published by The Arbinger Institute, is a modern version of the question/answer/discussion approach, and is, admittedly, a quite interesting study.

That said, having read hundreds of books about leadership, I have grown tired of trite sayings attempting to define it on a bumper sticker: "You manage things but lead people." Okay, so what? To lead means to take somebody somewhere. Okay, this is obvious. What else is obvious? It is obvious that the leader cannot exist without the followers. The opposite is not necessarily true. The followers can benefit from a leader's direction and wisdom, but they do not need him or her to exist. Understanding this relationship between leader and follower places the role of the leader in the proper perspective. Allow me to cherry-pick a sentence or two from the ancient Chinese military classic *The Methods of the Ssu-ma*, dating to approximately the fourth century BCE: "If you lead in person they will follow. When orders are annoying they will be ignored."[2] Or from Sun-tzu's *Art of War*, dating to the fifth to sixth century BCE: "When the troops continually gather in small groups and whisper together, the general has lost the confidence of the army."[3]

Although it should be obvious, as Bubba said, that it is the leader's job to figure out what makes the team tick, this detail was conveniently overlooked when an overly zealous manager at a company for which Bubba worked posted signs that read, "Goals Under Construction," and proceeded to hang miniature hardhats in the door openings to the various offices and work areas. The team was not happy. Rather than enthusiastically "constructing" his goals and entering a competition for the "Grand Prize," whatever it might have been, Bubba went home looking sullen and started searching for a new job. When he told me this story, it became dismally clear to me that goals cannot solely be the company's goals or the manager's goals; they must be the team's goals and as such the goals of each individual member of the team. Adrian Gostick and Chester Elton, authors of *The Carrot Principle*, remind us that "[s]urprisingly, many leaders think their job of pursuing a central goal ends once the company values are written. 'We printed wallet cards; everybody got one. And we've made sure each conference room has a framed poster with the values,' a leader once told us. Then the leaders seem surprised when the people's behavior does not conform to the organization's stated values."[4]

Although leadership books and popular slogans such as, "Today is the first day of the rest of your life," or, "half-full is better than half-empty," can aid thinking, when reality contradicts theory, you should go with reality. Reality in leadership is often what your gut tells you and not what you wish for, nor what some mathematical equation or scientific principle suggests. The logic of leadership is grounded in empirical evidence of right or wrong behavior, and, yes, the leader must face a level of personal risk. A leader who is so passionate about an idea that it brings him to tears may momentarily touch some hearts, but he will rarely win the minds of his team without demonstrating the will to inconvenience himself for his cause. Moreover, successful leadership requires a holistic approach supported by innovative ideas. But the ability to know how to think rather than what to think may be the leader's greatest asset. Learning how to think involves a conscious element of skepticism. It requires awareness of biases related to previous experiences, strong personal views, or current ambitions.

The leader's first responsibility when attempting to express a vision, solve a problem, reach a consensus, and lead the team toward the goal is therefore to define reality; to think critically, encourage response, and avoid getting trapped in meaningless sayings. Chinese statesman and military leader Deng Xiaoping

(1904-1997 CE) informed us that debate tends to make things "complicated."[5] He was right, of course, but likely had only his own interests in mind. The fact that your followers do not accept an atmosphere of strict obedience should be celebrated. If you can draw strength from their resourcefulness, you will welcome doubt without viewing it as an assault on your person. In fact, a healthy dose of talk and debate can have the effect of bringing down barriers, not raising them.

At its core leadership is about understanding human nature. Adolf Hitler (1889-1945 CE), in *Mein Kampf*, spoke about the "small measure of thinking power the broad masses possess,"[6] thereby reminding us that understanding human nature is also an essential key to controlling it. Cringe if you will at my use of a quote from he who is perhaps the most despised man in modern history. But being clever, even insightful, is not synonymous with having an admirable character. Hitler was right. Had the masses utilized their thinking power properly, there is a good chance that the Holocaust would not have happened. He also said, "I found it difficult to understand how men who always had reasonable ideas when they spoke as individuals with one another suddenly lost this reasonableness the moment they acted in the mass."[7] It is called groupthink in modern lingo, and tends to occur within a group of people who are trying to reach a consensus without applying critical thought and analysis. Joseph Goebbels (1897-1945 CE), Hitler's minister of propaganda, understood that any mantra repeated often enough is apt to become viewed as true. Thus without a proper understanding of human nature, ranting about how there is no "I" in team and together everybody achieves more could have dangerous consequences. The dissenters, those who question your ideas, may be your most valuable employees because they counteract this groupthink mentality and help you achieve a more balanced perspective.

Let me admit at the outset that unlike many leadership studies this book takes an analytical rather than motivational tack that is meant to stir at least some controversy, and the purpose of which is to incite the reader to be honest with himself or herself when attempting to establish a leadership approach that works with his or her team. When you understand human nature and your mind is free of clutter, you can ask the right questions that will inevitably guide you to the right answers. You can then speak the truth with conviction and inspire others to follow. But remember that any search for truth requires skepticism. This book is therefore equally much about provoking the follower to think about how to recognize and sabotage, if he or she chooses, manipulative leadership behavior aimed, as Hitler suggested, at the "small measure of thinking power the broad masses possess."

Just as physical courage may be the first characteristic of good generalship on the battlefield, moral courage is the first characteristic of good leadership in the civilian world and includes taking full responsibility for your actions. Many supervisors show an aptitude for risk taking because of their personal career ambitions. We therefore call them courageous. Yet having the moral courage to stand by the actions of the team when placed under scrutiny by management is a trait that many supervisors lack, because they fully know that moving to higher pay or a greater bonus requires only that they please their superiors. (How often would the supervisors at your place of employment be promoted to higher positions if promotions relied solely on the recommendations of the employees? This would in essence mean that the supervisors must make an effort to please their subordinates.) By contrast, a good leader is the assistant to the team and is simultaneously at the mercy of the team. He gives the team the benefit of the doubt while risking the mistakes and blunders. The question to ponder is this: At what point does the price become greater than the value, and how do you balance the two to ensure that you reach your objective without losing the respect of your team? "Climb if you will," said British climber and explorer Edward Whymper (1840-1911 CE), "but remember that courage and strength are naught without prudence, and a momentary negligence may destroy the happiness of a lifetime."[8]

As evidenced by the immensely large number of leadership books on the market, one tends to think that leadership is a profound subject that needs this much coverage in order that one can make sense of it. "In 1975 two hundred books were published on the subject of managing and leading. By 1997 that number had more than tripled. In fact, over the last twenty years authors have offered up over nine thousand different systems, languages, principles, and paradigms to help explain the mysteries of management and leadership."[9] But many modern ideas about leadership are nothing but hybrids of older ideas, and rarely is an idea truly new. In fact, as American journalist Robert D. Kaplan (1952- CE) observed, "Some truths are so obvious that to mention them in polite company seems either pointless or rude. What is left unstated, however, can with time be forgotten."[10] The purpose of this book is to conduct a critical analysis of leadership principles while simultaneously remind the reader of the obvious. To accomplish this objective, I will rely on three common leadership models for support which I call Leading with War; Leading with Cheese, Fish, and Carrots; and Leading with Science. That which is less obvious will then be dissected until the hidden truths are revealed; the small intangible parts that are often overlooked in the numerous motivational leadership studies on the market.

This book is thus not so much about leadership per se, as it is about how to think about leadership by learning to ask the appropriate questions and learning to find the appropriate answers. My hope is that the examples I offer will resonate with the reader, providing him or her with deeper insights into the trends that shape the growing number of leadership books on the market. You can choose to grow your bad habits or your good habits for future generation leaders to study. Neither way necessarily requires more effort than the other, but it does require the wisdom to know the difference. You will not always get it precisely right; however, you should also not be too far wrong. After all, leadership ain't rocket science!

Part I

Leading with War

"Experience is of more value in the Art of War than all philosophical truth."

— Carl von Clausewitz

"How fortunate for leaders that men do not think."

— Adolf Hitler

"No man is good enough to govern another man, without that other's consent."

— Abraham Lincoln

THE GREAT GENERALS

Some say that war, however brutal and disgusting we may find it, brings out the finest qualities in leaders: courage, honor, integrity, and, above all, character. The lessons of war have come to serve as popular civilian leadership models. Consider for a moment how leaders on every level of the corporate ladder are likely to identify with the widely quoted *Art of War*, an ancient military text and classic work on strategy by Chinese general and philosopher Sun-tzu (c. 544-496 BCE): "One who knows the enemy and knows himself will not be endangered in a hundred engagements,"[11] or, "Attaining one hundred victories in one hundred battles is not the pinnacle of excellence. Subjugating the enemy's army without fighting is the true pinnacle of excellence."[12] On the home front Robert E. Lee (1807-1870 CE) might be more celebrated than any other American Civil War hero. His character, compassion, and cunning ability to thwart his foes and lead the Confederacy against the Union in what ultimately became a losing battle has been studied, written about, commented upon, and quoted in texts too numerous to mention. Should we study the great generals of history and Lead with War?

Before answering, think about this: To what extent is it true to say that great military leaders are necessarily compassionate with respect to their subordinates or the opposition, or strive to take the ethically high road of winning without fighting? Richard Marcinko (1940- CE) (a.k.a. the Rogue Warrior), former United States Navy SEAL and author of *Leadership Secrets of the Rogue Warrior*, put it simply when he said, "Thou shalt win at all cost,"[13] and, "To survive and succeed, you must accept one plain and painful truth: Business can be war. Life can be war. If you want to win that war: Attack. Attack! ATTACK!"[14] Napoleon Bonaparte (1769-1821 CE), military and political leader during the French Revolution, would have agreed. He saw only one thing—the enemy's main body—and tried to crush it, confident that secondary matters would settle themselves.

As we shall see, leaders and leadership principles are full of contradictions, as reflected in the views of military strategists and generals the world over. For example, as stated by ancient Chinese military strategist Zhuge Liang (181-234 CE), "Military authority, directing the armed forces, is the matter of the authoritative power of the leading general. If the general can hold the authority of the military and operate its power, he oversees his subordinates like a fierce tiger with wings, flying over the four seas, going into action whenever there is an encounter."[15] Contrast his views with United States Army retired Lieutenant General Russel L. Honoré's (1947-CE) opinion that leadership does not simply involve barking orders and expecting results. Even an organization such as the army, where soldiers supposedly are committed to following orders, must remember that people are people first before they are soldiers or subordinates. Even if soldiers have no choice but to follow orders, they still have the power to affect the outcome. The leader should therefore "set people on the right path" rather than boss them, and, according to General Honoré, "do the planning and then to motivate the execution."[16]

A particularly important observation might be General Honoré's view that "[l]eaders should keep dissenters close because they'll provide a valuable perspective."[17] Failing to create a sense of purpose behind the mission will make it difficult to reach efficiency. Unless the team has the proper equipment to execute the plan, no motivation in the world will move them to action. "I was always fond of logistics, even though I was an infantry officer," says Honoré. "So I would drive all my organizations crazy about logistics because logistics was always the hardest thing to get done. So many times units failed, not because they weren't capable but because they didn't get the gas, the boots, and the bullets on time."[18] Can you identify an occasion at your place of employment when you were unable to be as efficient as you would have liked because you could not get the proper equipment to function, or did not have access to the equipment you needed?

Although it is obvious that one can catch more flies with sugar than vinegar, and military personnel as well as employees in the civilian world are less likely to backfire when they believe in the value of the principles they are subjected to, the best way to treat one's subordinates, whether or not to listen to and value their advice and suggestions, appears to be a highly individual matter. As underscored by a former King of Prussia, Frederick the Great

(1712-1786 CE), "The general [should] talk of war from time to time with the most enlightened generals of his army . . . and if, in free conversation, they offer good advice, he should profit by it without remarking who has found a good thing; but once it is executed with success, he should say, in the presence of a big group of officers: It is to so-and-so that I owe the success in this affair."[19] Yet on the same subject and in nearly the same era Napoleon said, "In military operations, I consulted no one but myself."[20] American President Abraham Lincoln (1809-1865 CE), who guided America through the devastating experience of the Civil War, supposedly took a different middle of the road type approach: "He met with his generals and cabinet members in their homes, offices, and in the field, principally to provide direction and leadership. He toured the Navy Yard and the fortifications in and around Washington, and inspected new weaponry, all to obtain accurate knowledge of the workings and abilities of the armed forces. This contact also gave him the first-hand knowledge he needed to make informed, accurate decisions without having to rely solely on the word of others."[21] Who was right? Who was the better leader?

What we can learn from these examples is that there are different perspectives on leadership that we tend to cherry-pick as we see fit. Yes, we admire Robert E. Lee because he had character and led from the front with purpose and direction, motivating and instilling pride in those he led, as relayed in this account by H. W. Crocker III:

> If Lee respected the rights of his superiors, he also respected his subordinates. For one thing, he treated them as adults. His method of leadership was far removed from the childish ersatz challenges and rewards contemporary managers like to dangle before their employees—selecting managers-of-the-month, gathering self-conscious "team" cheerleading sessions, organizing weekend whitewater rafting or mountain climbing to teach "leadership" and "teamwork". . . A business should be what the Army of Northern Virginia was: a

"voluntary association of gentlemen organized for the sole purpose" of one's enterprise. That purpose is best achieved, and one's subordinates are best inspired, by doing, not by playing games and offering carnival prizes.[22]

But while we admire Robert E. Lee for his character, we simultaneously admire Napoleon, not because of his character, but because he knew how to win. Winning matters perhaps even more than how one plays the game. To retain leadership a leader must succeed more often than he loses. But shalt thou really win at all cost, as stressed by the Rogue Warrior Richard Marcinko? Is business really war? In addition to requiring an enormous personal sacrifice from each member of his team, the Rogue Warrior might be too tough to stomach for most people. Not only does he agree with Friedrich Nietzsche's (1844-1900 CE) dictum, "Whatever does not break my back makes me stronger," but thinks that a manager should demand that his subordinates work so hard that it literally hurts. However, this is often not possible because in our "soft" world, as Marcinko suggests, such a manager would be "branded as a tyrant or sadist."[23]

So who is right: Robert E. Lee or Richard Marcinko? When attempting to answer this question, one might start by asking whether it is true that what does not break your back makes you stronger. The problem with making assumptions, says the Rogue Warrior, is that "when people assume things, they generally think that everyone else . . . is making the same assumptions."[24] Yet, he does just this—assume—when quoting Nietzsche's dictum. Few people would be willing to sacrifice their health, sleep, well-being, or family for their boss or company, even if the pain is more mental than physical in the civilian world of business. Are these people necessarily lazy and poor team players?

Although he has no doubt offered much insight into successful leadership strategies; for example, that one's vision must be "sensible, achievable, and personally rewarding" to inspire the employees to achieve it,[25] the Rogue Warrior's principles are full of contradictions not just when compared with those of civilian leaders, but when compared with statements made by other important military figures. For example, George Patton (1885-1945 CE), who the Rogue Warrior quoted, is perhaps best known for his leadership skills in commanding armies in World War II: "The time to take counsel of your fears is before you make an important battle decision . . . Any man who is afraid to die will never really live!"[26] But before you take this statement to heart, consider for a moment the views of the much celebrated United States Air Force test pilot Chuck Yeager (1923- CE), who broke the sound barrier in 1947: "I was always afraid of dying. Always. It was my fear that made me learn everything I could about my airplane and my emergency equipment, and kept me flying respectful of my machine and always alert in the cockpit. If you want to grow old as a pilot, you've got to know when to push it, and when to back off."[27]

Chuck Yeager was so afraid of dying that he could not afford to make mistakes. His views communicate the value attached to understanding one's capabilities and limitations. Richard Hiner, retired as vice president of training from the AOPA (Aircraft Owners and Pilots Association and Air Safety Foundation), stated the following in a newsletter in 2005:

> During a flight review, a well-seasoned pilot posed a question that I had never before been asked. "After all your hours in the air, do you still get butterflies in your stomach when you climb into the cockpit?" "Yes," I responded, "and if they ever go away, I'll stop flying." This pilot thought that a little fear and anxiety was a sign of weakness or a lack of skill, something to be avoided. Au contraire, I told him; it keeps you sharp, gives you an edge, and causes you to check and recheck the airplane, the weather, and your own physical and mental condition before taking to the air. A little fear and anxiety is something to be encouraged, not resisted.[28]

What should be learned from these examples is that it is healthy to ask what can be achieved at your particular place on the leadership ladder. As Norse historian Snorri Sturluson (1178-1241 CE) reminded us nearly a millennium ago, "Consider with thyself what thou art man enough to undertake . . . for to take up great resolutions, and then to lay them aside, would only end in dishonor."[29] Thus when the price becomes greater than the value, it is prudent to cut your losses and run. In his book, *A First-Rate Madness: Uncovering the Links Between Leadership and Mental Illness*, Nassir Ghaemi reminds us that "an excess of virtue is a vice," and advises us to "recall that the classical Greek concept of virtue, derived from Aristotle, involved moderation":

> Too much virtue converts courage to recklessness, for instance. It may be legitimate to turn around and flee, rather than fight, under the right circumstances. That is what Aristotle meant by virtue, not some ideal of never-changing steadfastness. Given this perspective, one cannot cleanly separate virtue from vice, for the virtue of courage sometimes involves fighting, sometimes retreating, sometimes charging—each action interpretable as vices of violence, cowardice, and recklessness.[30]

Leadership is not war, nor is business war as claimed by the Rogue Warrior. Leadership and business are not wars any more than the war on drugs or the war on illiteracy are wars. *Thou shalt not win at all cost, lest thou might score a pyrrhic victory when the opposition rises up to smite thee.* There is more to success than Attack. Attack! ATTACK! The Rogue Warrior's "missions were deadly and difficult," which placed him in position to "expect nothing less from [his] men than total dedication and absolute competence."[31] But if you want to use the underlying principles of attack in non-deadly business endeavors, you cannot take them literally. Although leadership is about character (or to extend the cliché: Leadership is to *have* character but not *be* a character), it is NOT about flattering yourself over your ability to think up clever slogans. And even character cannot win if the strategy is poor, as demonstrated in the following example:

The impeachment of [President] Bill Clinton over his affair with Monica Lewinsky, a White House intern, brought forth years of pontification on sex and politics. The implication was, for Clinton critics, that a good president had to display "good character"—kindness, moral rectitude, self-control, and so on. "Character above all" became the mantra (the title, for instance, of a PBS broadcast subtitled "An Exploration of Presidential Leadership." [Yet] journalist Ronald Kessler titled his sympathetic biography of [President George W.] Bush "A Matter of Character," and emphasized how Bush's superior behavior made him a better leader than Clinton. Bush had more sexual continence than Clinton; he may have been better behaved with staff; he may have been more normal and decent. But all that might argue against, not for, better leadership skills as a president in time of crisis.[32]

Which view you take may be a matter of your political stand. However, to make the best use of the insights that the great historical generals offer us (and of the insights offered by journalists and lay people as well), we must watch for source bias, place their views in proper perspective, and understand that the information must be modified to be used successfully within our own particular organization. Let us look at a few historical accounts of warfare from the perspectives of the generals and the soldiers. As you read these brief summaries, consider whether or not you would have liked to serve in these wars under these leaders. What makes you tick and what doesn't, and why? If you desire to Lead with War, I would recommend reading these accounts in their entirety as a basic education in different leadership styles. Most of them are available for free online.

THUCYDIDES (c. 460-395 BCE)

Thucydides, a Greek historian and Athenian general, credited with writing the *History of the Peloponnesian War* between the Athens Empire and the Peloponnesian League led by Sparta in the fifth century BCE, believed that the twenty-seven year long conflict (431-404 BCE) with a six-year interlude of peace, which ended with Athens' surrender to Sparta, was one of the greatest wars that had taken place among the Greek, a belief he based on the examination of earlier wars: ". . . looking into times of past, I have yet light on to persuade me, I do not think they have been very great, either for matter of war or otherwise."[33]

Thucydides wrote from the perspective of a man directly involved in the war as opposed to reflecting on it after it had ended. But he was not an eye-witness to every event. So when interpreting the account, the historian must be aware of possible biases. Simultaneously Thucydides had a unique way of weighing one side of the conflict against the other and demonstrated little hope of winning the war for Athens. Since the conflict was one of the greatest that had taken place among the Greek, he found it crucial to relate it to future generations. His writings provide good insight into human nature and the difficulties of judging war objectively: "And though men always judge the present war wherein they live to be greatest, and when it is past, admire more those that were before it, yet if they consider of this war by the acts done in the same, it will manifest itself to be greater than any of those before mentioned."[34]

The uncertainty of life in Greece and the many enemy invasions created reluctance among the citizens to settle permanently and work the fields, and many left for Athens, the most potent and stable of all cities, which grew large as a result. Thucydides spends considerable time exploring Greek life and laying the foundation for the conflict. For example, he notes how houses were unfenced and traveling unsafe because thieves were crossing from one island to another. The people had to accustom themselves to wearing armor and building walls around their cities. He makes references to the taking of Troy, which demonstrates that he knew his history, and further educates the reader about the wealth of Greece, the wars fought between Athens and Aegina, one of the Greek islands, and the great power of the Greek navies that exercised dominion over other peoples.

Sparta, however, became a powerful enemy of Athens despite the fact that it was sparsely decorated and constructed with scattered villages and, thus, to an observer would seem the least powerful of the two and definitely inferior to Athens. The Athenians and the Spartans divided themselves into leagues, the Athenians with command of the sea and the Spartans with command of the land. The dangers experienced in the long lasting war sharpened the military edge of both Athens and Sparta. Yet Thucydides admits that it was difficult to know the certainty of what took place, because many people had spoken of many things. For example, of the long speeches of the assembly between the Corinthians and the Corcyraeans which are related in the *History of the Peloponnesian War*, one speech covers a full seven pages and is unlikely accurate word for word, although it may well be accurate in overall content.

On several occasions Thucydides demonstrates how victory is subjective: First the Corinthians set up a trophy. Then the Corcyraeans, "as if they had the victory, set up a trophy likewise."[35] The Corinthians believed they were victorious, because they had caused more destruction and killed more of the enemy. The Corcyraeans believed they were victorious, because they had sunk thirty galleys of the Corinthians and recovered many dead bodies, and also because the Corinthians had the previous day rowed away from them, which could be viewed either as an act of cowardice or defeat. Thucydides also provides good insight into how Sparta justified the war against Athens, which is particularly interesting because of his position as an Athenian general. For example, he relates how Sthenelaidas stood up and spoke to the Lacedaemonians (Spartans) about the actions of the Athenians:

> For though they have been much in their own
> praises, yet they have said nothing to the contrary
> but that they have done injury to our confederates . .
> . Let no man tell me that after we have once
> received injury we ought to deliberate. No, it

belongs rather to the doers of injury to spend time in consultation. Wherefore, men of Lacedaemon, decree the war, as becometh the dignity of Sparta; and let not the Athenians grow yet greater, nor let us betray our confederates, but in the name of the Gods proceed against the doers of injustice.[36]

Additionally, the Lacedaemonians, the ambassadors of the several confederates, and the Corinthians spoke to the effect:

For though it be the part of discreet men to be quiet unless they have wrong, yet it is the part of valiant men, when they receive injury, to pass from peace into war, and after success, from war to come again to composition, and neither to swell with the good success of war not to suffer injury through pleasure taken in the ease of peace.[37]

History supposedly informs the actions of the future leadership. Yet Thucydides acknowledged that leadership cannot be based on historical events, and that leaders tend to distort the truth to benefit their particular aim. He believed that there are essentially three elements responsible for war: honor, fear, and interest. Going to war is honorable in the sense that a man fights for his state and its citizen, which allows him to build a reputation that distinguishes him from the masses; fear causes people to form into groups for common protection against enemies; and interest results from wanting something for personal gain. The challenges of war are many: "Consider before you enter how unexpected the chances of war be. For a long war for the most part endeth in calamity . . . And men, when they go to war, use many times to fall first to action . . . and when they have taken harm, then they fall to reasoning."[38] How often do you see in your own organization new ideas implemented with great enthusiasm but little forethought, and first when the leaders "have taken harm" do they "fall to reasoning"? Thucydides might have had an aversion to conflict, or he might just have been an insightful man. He also warns us: "For no man comes to execute a thing with the same confidence he premeditates it. For we deliver opinions in safety, whereas in the action itself we fail through fear."[39]

Although he understood the calamity brought by war, Thucydides simultaneously believed that if one is to retain power for future generations, then enemies must be resisted in any and every way. The natural law of humanity is that the weaker are subject to the stronger, and those who are stronger can naturally use their strength to force their subjects into compliance. Thus the strong do what they can and the weak suffer what they must. Tyrants, who are often the heads of states or the leaders in war, tend to provide only for themselves, their own comfort, and the aggrandizement of their immediate family. Needless to say, this sort of self-aggrandizement among the leadership creates injustices and tends to sabotage the subordinates' willingness to follow. In a civilian business where the subordinates generally have more say than in the army, a tyrant leader would have difficulty bringing his team to action.

Thucydides further observes that when the leadership is just, a great tower of strength can be created even when the populace must sacrifice. Kindness, when shown at the proper time, has great power to remove grievances that would otherwise stand in one's way and sabotage the team's motivation to pursue the goal. From Athenian statesman Pericles' (c. 495-429 BCE) funeral oration delivered at the end of the first year of the Peloponnesian War, we can deduce that it is crucial that ordinary citizens occupy themselves with the affairs of the state:

> Our public men have, besides politics, their private affairs to attend to, and our ordinary citizens, though occupied with the pursuits of industry, are still fair judges of public matters; for, unlike any other nation, regarding him who takes no part in these duties not as unambitious but as useless, we Athenians are able to judge at all events if we cannot originate, and instead of looking on discussion as a stumbling-block in the way of action, we think it an indispensable preliminary to any wise action at all.[40]

How can the ideas in this speech be applied to leadership in today's civilian workplace? If the employees take no interest in the affairs of the company for which they work, they become useless (or nearly so) to the company. And, as Pericles notes, debate and discussion should not be viewed as a stumbling-block in the way of action, but as a crucial necessity to wise action.

Furthermore, the Athenians compared themselves to their rivals, the Spartans, who in essence took their young from the cradle and, using iron discipline, educated them in matters of war. The Athenians, by contrast, would live exactly as they pleased, and yet were "just as ready to encounter every legitimate danger."[41] So how do we know just how much discipline the leadership should exercise on their subordinates to remain effective in reaching their goals? In Sparta every man was a soldier and owed strict obedience to the state, while in Athens life was more lenient. Yet both Sparta and Athens were great states that had the potential for great accomplishments.

The strength of Thucydides' account lies in his observations of human nature, and many of his ideas, although nearly two thousand five hundred years old, could as well have been written today. Not much has changed. Few are those who view current events with a critical eye, he notes. Rather than questioning and investigating various claims of "truth," we tend to readily accept whatever story is handed to us through tradition. Consider in your own organization the leadership's fondness of popular sayings intended to inspire the employees. Yet neither the leadership nor the employees typically spend more than the briefest of moments (if that) to question the validity of such slogans as, "You manage things but lead people." These slogans are used not necessarily because they speak the truth, but because they are attractive at truth's expense.

Thucydides also stresses inexperience or lack of insight as the common factors that make people eager to take up arms. In civilian leadership, are we not more prone to go along with new ideas that we have not fully discussed or thought about while we are still young and inexperienced? As we get older, we know more, think more, rely more on past experiences, and therefore frequently become more resistant to change. Many of Thucydides' insights thus seem well suited for modern inspirational books about leadership. But to use them in earnest, they must be examined in deeper context. If we "admire more those [wars] that were before," do we really have a clear perspective on the conflicts of our own time? And, if not, how can we use historical wisdom to gain that perspective?

XENOPHON (c. 431-354 BCE)

The March Up Country is the report of Xenophon's return from Persia where he has been aiding Cyrus the Younger in an attempt to take the throne from Cyrus' own brother, Artaxerxes II. In this detailed and with few exceptions trustworthy account of the Greek mercenaries' long march back to the sea, Xenophon, the protagonist of the story, an Athenian soldier and a pupil and admirer of Socrates, is elected to a leadership position after the death of Cyrus the Younger. Serving alongside of Cheirisophos, the commanding officer, he leads the Greek mercenaries, known as the Ten Thousand, through hostile territory to the Black Sea. Written objectively in clear prose that lacks splendor and exaggeration, the account describes the rigors, difficult terrain and weather, and the troops' encounters with enemy forces. The account is considered a classical historical work. Perhaps what makes it particularly unique is that the events the mercenaries encounter during the march portray no major battles but picture the army in defeat.

Since the army is constantly challenged by the enemy, Xenophon has several opportunities to act on his leadership skills. The first noteworthy mention is his professionalism in the form of strong and fair leadership. Always ready to listen to his troops, he is a passionate but realistic leader who employs an open-door policy where "anyone might come to him, at breakfast or supper, or if he slept could awake him, and tell anything he had to propose for the war."[42] Although self-critical in the analysis of his skills, he portrays himself as a slightly more just leader than Cheirisophos, who lashes out and strikes a guide in anger; an act of violence, which Xenophon describes as carelessness and perhaps the fundamental difference between himself and Cheirisophos. How Xenophon handles the difficulties related to motivating the tired, hungry, and cold troops is another testament to his compassion and ability as a leader. He starts by begging the weary troops not to stay behind as the enemy is on the chase. But when the men, too tired to move, ask that he cut their throats instead and go on without them, for "march they could not," he succumbs to their wishes to settle down for the night, "without fire or food, after posting such guards as he could."[43]

Each segment of the march, broken into measurements of stages and leagues, provides vivid images of the terrain and weather. When the troops get over the height where Tiribazos, the lieutenant-governor of Southern Armenia, means to attack them, they march "three desert stages, 15 leagues," and reach the River Euphrates which they cross "waist-deep," then move on through deep snow with a north wind blowing in their faces.[44] Xenophon's insightful details of the hardships they encounter can be described only by someone who has been there and done that. The insulating powers of the snow, for example, "kept them snug and warm where they lay unless it slipt off."[45] Good advice to help the poor state of the troops is given without exaggeration: The blinding effect of the snow is countered by holding "something black before their eyes," and frostbite is handled by taking their shoes off at night, for the newly flayed raw leather straps from untanned hides would otherwise work its way into their feet when the shoes froze.[46]

Xenophon's thoughtful strategic battle considerations add realism and credibility to the account. Prisoners are taken alive to act as guides, and language barriers are bridged with the help of interpreters. Great attention to detail is employed when describing the problems of defense during river crossings: "They could not go through the river in arms, or else the river carried them off; they could not carry the arms on their heads, or they were bare against arrows and other missiles."[47] The enemy is portrayed in simple and objective terms as "very good bowmen" with considerable skill at constructing strong weapons that could penetrate both shield and corselet. War casualties are acknowledged and the dead given "all the honours customary for brave men, as far as possible."[48]

When the morale of the Hellenes dwindles, leaving them without hope, Xenophon looks for alternate and more suitable routes to help men and animals pass with greater ease, or as an option, place the troops above the enemy on higher and more favorable ground. He offers ready answers to Cheirisophos' problems by suggesting that they not fight the enemy in lines but in company columns, which attests to his concern for the morale and safety of the men. A line will break at once due to the difficulty of the mountain terrain, he reasons, and such a break would demoralize the men and endanger the whole group. Instead, he suggests, the columns can come to the aid of one another and create difficulties for an enemy attempting to penetrate the spaces between them. The strongest should go on first, and the columns should be placed so far apart that the "extreme columns overlap the enemy wings."[49] A great deal of thought has obviously been afforded the issue of teamwork.

However, the detailed and matter-of-fact style of the writing lacks emotion and greater drama, and very little is told about the individual persons making up the Ten Thousand. In fact, the greatest dramatic moment may come when they finally observe the sea at Trebizond. The account as a whole is particularly interesting considering the fact that it portrays the actions taken after defeat rather than victory. The reactions of the men to the sight of the Black Sea, and the welcoming provisions of their countrymen in the Hellenic city of Euxine in the Colchian country, may be viewed as a victory in itself. Xenophon's memory of some of the details of the story can be questioned, considering that he wrote it sometime after his exile from Athens. His use of dream interpretation to determine the course of action seems a bit contrary to his otherwise brilliant leadership skills. But the reliance on dreams in story telling frequently comes in handy in ancient literature when few other options remain.

When studying *The March Up Country*, one might keep in mind that Xenophon was not just another soldier; he was in a leadership position and elected to this role when the Ten Thousand Greek were without a leader in hostile territory. Might his leadership role have influenced his desire for victory or how he portrayed the difficulties they encountered including the morale of the men? Might it have forced him to analyze events and think of solutions? Or might it have made him trivialize the difficulties so that the men would appear stronger than they were to convey a more positive account for future generations? Despite the fact that some historians like to place this ancient narrative in the "Great Man" category (implying that successes are largely determined by a single human being—a great man—and not by political or environmental circumstances), my view is that the text as a whole seems honest, avoids exaggeration, and examines the boundaries of human capability. As an autobiographical account written from a third person perspective, it is largely void of opinion or emotion.

JULIUS CAESAR (c. 100-44 BCE)

Julius Caesar was a Roman statesman and military leader with ambitions to conquer Gaul to extend his dominions and neutralize any threats against his empire. His reputation as a strong military leader and strategist is clearly demonstrated in *De Bello Gallico & Other Commentaries of Caius Julius Caesar*, and it is not for nothing that he took the title of dictator (one who gives orders). The story is recounted from the position of a man who is clearly offense/attack oriented and finds it "better to be slain in battle than not to recover [our] ancient glory in war."[50] At times he is bold to the point of being reckless. The *Commentaries* start by giving the reasons for the unrest: Gaul was entering into a confederacy against the Roman people because they feared that the Roman army would be led against them. The fact that the Roman army passed the winter in Gaul caused a great deal of concern among the Gallic people and some were anxious for a revolution.

The *Commentaries* are easy to read, full of graphic description, and rich in detail regarding battle strategies, architectures of forts and walls, and descriptions of battlegrounds. For example, "A hill, declining evenly from the top, extended to the river Sambre," which depth was about three feet, and a second hill "of like ascent . . . and open from about 200 paces at the lowest part; but in the upper part, woody . . . [made it] not easy to see through it."[51] When organizing for battle, the standard is displayed signaling the necessity to run to arms, with signal also given by trumpet to call the soldiers back who had left to seek materials for the rampart. When the battle order is formed, the soldiers are encouraged and watchword given. The battle organization described in the account reinforces the idea that the soldiers were largely self-reliant and able to teamwork to take advantage of opportunities as they arose. "[H]aving been trained by former engagements," the soldiers could suggest to themselves what to do, making it possible to proceed without a leader present at every moment: "[O]n account of the near approach and the speed of the enemy, [they] did not then wait for any command from Caesar."[52] The strategy consists of dividing the forces of the enemy, "so that it might not be necessary to engage with so large a number at one time."[53]

Caesar inquires of the hostages and captives to collect information about the enemy. Information is also carried to him through scouts and letters. He portrays a rather negative image of enemy discipline, as he observes the enemy "marching out of their camp at the second watch, with great noise and confusion, in no fixed order, nor under any command, since each sought for himself the foremost place in the journey, and hastened to reach home, they made their departure appear very like a flight."[54] The cavalry of the Treviri, a tribe of the Gauls, whose reputation for courage is extraordinary, is much alarmed, but when they see the Roman camp filled with enemy forces, hard pressed, they hasten home to relate that the Romans have been conquered.

Caesar also balances this negative account by describing the enemy as having such great courage that "when the foremost of them had fallen, the next stood upon them . . . and fought from their bodies," and those who survived "cast their weapons against our men, as from a mound [of dead bodies]."[55] Simultaneously he portrays himself in a good light and praises his soldiers. For example, when addressing the legions, he does so one by one. When he says he "would raise the siege, if they felt the scarcity too severely, they unanimously begged him not to do so; that they had served for several years under his command in such manner, that they never submitted to insult, and never abandoned an enterprise without accomplishing it; that they should consider it a disgrace if they abandoned the siege after commencing it."[56] One wonders if this is really the words of the legions, or Caesar's own words trying to paint a picture of greater support than he had.

Critognatus, a Gallic noble holds an interesting speech about the disgracefulness of surrender, even as supplies are running short: "To be unable to bear privation for a short time is disgraceful cowardice, not true valour. Those who voluntarily offer themselves to death are more easily found than those who would calmly endure distress . . . What courage do you think would our relatives and friends have, if eighty thousand men were butchered in one spot."[57] Did Caesar learn a valuable lesson in leadership from pondering his enemy's speech when he said that "[i]t is easier to find men who will volunteer to die, than to find those who are willing to endure pain with patience"?

In regards to counting war casualties, it would have been interesting to know how many men Caesar lost. He describes the enemy losses as quite severe. When the enemy surrenders and sends ambassadors to Caesar, and recounts the calamity of their state, "their senators were reduced from 600 to three; that from 60,000 men they were reduced to scarcely 500 who could bear arms"[58]

Overall, Caesar comes across as a rather unpleasant personality to friend and foe alike. He shows little compassion for the troops. For example, he "censure[s] the rashness and avarice of his soldiers" and accuses them of being arrogant, "because they thought that they knew more than their general concerning victory, and the issue of actions: and that he required in his soldiers forbearance and self-command, not less than valour and magnanimity."[59] His harshness is in stark contrasts to the accounts of Thucydides and Xenophon. Despite his unpleasant appearance, however, Caesar does take the time to recognize his lieutenants by naming them. For example, Quintus Pedius, Lucius Aurunculeius Cotta, and Titus Labienus are mentioned in the text.[60] He motivates the troops by proposing "a reward for those who should first scale the walls."[61] I question, however, whether Caesar really was as observant to non-military detail as is described. His account of how "the matrons begin to cast their clothes and silver over the wall, and bending over as far as the lower part of their bosom, with outstretched hands,"[62] certainly gives a vivid image that entertains the reader, but to what extent is it true?

JOHANN VON EWALD (1744-1813 CE)

Let us jump forward a couple of thousand years to near modern day. The diary of Johann von Ewald, a Hessian infantry officer from the Germanic regiments who fought for the English in the American Revolutionary War, is a touching eye-opener for those desiring to experience the American triumph as seen from the viewpoint of the opposition. The diary, covering the period between 1776 and 1784, appears to have been written systematically at the end of each day, until Ewald fell ill and missed recording several months of events. The day-by-day writings are delivered in short segments recording the happenings of morning, afternoon, and evening, and as such present an easy to read first-person view of the war translated into modern English.

The basic and rather non-analytic recounts of events display little emotion initially and, although many details are expressed, fail to give the reader a good visual image of the happenings. For example, Ewald records that his regiment took several casualties, but says nothing about how these men died or how their deaths affected the morale of the troops. When losing a very good friend, he simply states that he regretted the loss. Occasionally, when Ewald observes the enemy, the descriptions become more vivid: "[W]e ran into two riflemen at a bend in the road who, because of the hard rain and wind behind us, had their faces so hidden under their round hats that they were not aware of us."[63] This seems to indicate that Ewald preferred to articulate the observations he made of the enemy rather than embark on a more introspective journey of his own regiment.

The men in Ewald's regiment were mainly recruited in Germany and hired out by the German leaders. Because of their status as foreign conscripts fighting for the English, the Hessian soldiers probably did not earn a significant salary. One might wonder how motivated they were to pursue the war. It seems reasonable, as Ewald states, that they "wanted to spare the King's subjects and hoped to terminate the war amicably,"[64] but he also seems frustrated with the delay of the English: "I see, they do not want to finish the war!"[65] His comment reinforces the belief that motivation to fight was rather slim for the Hessian soldiers. On

41

several occasions Ewald displays empathy for the enemy, for example, when trying to convince the people of the plantation where he is staying that there is, in fact, humane persons in the Hessian army: To "invite their good will and gratitude" he "gave them every protection."[66] However, he also shows signs of arrogance when laughing in the face of the town councilor of Burlington, perhaps as a result of his recent successful patrol, attributed to stormy weather, which precluded the enemy parties from crossing the road. He seems to find pleasure in the opportunity to identify himself as a Hessian soldier to the tenants of a house, telling them they are his prisoners: "The ladies fell at my knees and begged me to leave them their husbands."[67]

The diary becomes particularly absorbing when Ewald receives the message of George Washington's surprise attack on the regiments on the day after Christmas, and "a second messenger of doom arrived, confirming the report and adding that all had been taken prisoner."[68] Ewald's opinion that "the fate of entire kingdoms often depend upon a few blockheads of irresolute men," presents an interesting revelation about the English leadership.[69] He is clearly disgusted with how the English army has been "put to such poor use that eight campaigns were lost" and "thirteen provinces" which has "torn down the Crown of England from its loftiest peak."[70] A wonderful analogy is made when Ewald realizes the reversal of his fate: Four weeks ago, the English had expected to win the war and now "had to render Washington the honor of thinking about our defense." Since the English army had so underestimated their enemy, such fright came over the men that "from this unhappy day onward we saw everything through a magnifying glass."[71]

A curious shift in the way the events are recorded takes place in the supplement to the diary, after the peace is concluded and the United States has been declared independent. Now that the war is over, the diary becomes more introspective and, as a result, the reader can easily identify both with the Americans and Ewald, and with that idea of "Liberty and Independence" for which the Americans were willing to "have their arms and legs smashed."[72] Ewald starts by recounting the losses of the war and, while waiting his turn to ship back home, takes the opportunity to journey to

West Point. It becomes obvious that he harbors certain awe for the badly supplied American forces that stubbornly refused to give in to the English. The comparison made between the American army "in its wretched condition," and the "splendid and formidable army of the English"[73] during Ewald's visit to West Point is especially revealing. The men on the parade ground "looked haggard and pallid and were poorly dressed. Indeed, very many stood quite proudly under arms without shoes and stockings,"[74] and officers who had "marched without shoes . . . still did everything that was possible to live in this world as free men."[75]

When the time comes for Ewald to board the ship and leave for Europe, he displays real longing for the "new country," where on all corners the flag of thirteen stripes is flying and the shores are crowded with people throwing their hats in the air and screaming with joy. The final blow comes when Ewald returns home and fails to receive recognition for the eight years he has spent abroad fighting a war that, in his opinion, was unwinnable. All "services performed were forgotten" and the Hessian soldiers were forced to bend their "proud backs under everything, because it could not be otherwise."[76]

Overall, the insights displayed in Johann von Ewald's diary are deep and appear truthful. For example, when one has nothing left to lose and nothing more to gain, one does what one must do. Ewald believed that Washington, despite the wretched condition of his troops, "would still undertake something, especially when he was in a position to lose everything otherwise."[77] The diary—displaying two continents, two peoples, but separated perhaps by more than the distance of an ocean—certainly gives the reader the opportunity to experience the spirit of the military practices of the time. After the end of the war, many Hessian soldiers remained in America. A large number had also died during the war, either in action or from disease. Ewald recorded the losses of the Hessian Corps alone in numbers nearing 6,000. The diary is a good book for those Americans who would like to experience their triumph as seen through the eyes of the opposition.

ARMAND DE CAULAINCOURT (1773-1827 CE)

Before his fall from power, and despite what in some people's eyes was a laughable physical stature of merely five feet two inches, Napoleon Bonaparte managed to reach astounding successes in his military campaigns and was thereby able to rise to magnificent heights as ruler of large parts of Western Europe. Although Napoleon is said to have been able to inspire others because he had such a fine sense of the impact that morale had on warfare, not all who served under him agreed. The memoirs by Armand de Caulaincourt, who served under Napoleon during his disastrous campaign into Russia in 1812, read like a novel and discuss Caulaincourt's relationship with the Emperor in a way that indicates that he had intimate knowledge of Napoleon's thoughts. Napoleon relied on Caulaincourt's opinions of how to proceed; although, according to Caulaincourt, "the Emperor delivered a rapid fire of questions and of the answers that he wished to hear," as a result of his hunger for battle.[78] Napoleon also proved gloomy when he feared that the Russian army might escape him, and that he might not, "for some time, obtain the battle he desired so keenly."[79]

Entering the army at fifteen years of age, Armand de Caulaincourt served for a long time without achieving any significant rank. Eventually he rose in rank and went to St. Petersburg on Napoleon's insistence, where he was officially an ambassador but probably more likely a spy; although, spies were said to have been "useless from the moment we crossed on to Russian soil,"[80] which was also why prisoners who could supply information proved crucial. In fact, Napoleon considered the war inconclusive unless prisoners were taken, and "[s]everal times he asked, of the officers who came with reports of our successes, where the prisoners were who ought to have been captured."[81]

Napoleon went to Russia to "finish off, once and for all, the Colossus of Northern Barbarism," so that it would not "interfere with civilized Europe."[82] One might question, however, whether it really was his fear of barbarism and not the hunger for a campaign that made him go. Or as Caulaincourt states, "The Emperor was so anxious for a battle that he drove the army forward with all his energy."[83] Appearing to have wanted the war regardless of any advice he received to the contrary, Napoleon was beaming with pride at the opportunity to measure "his strength with the enemy and obtaining a result that should give some colour to his expedition."[84]

Napoleon's hunger for battle is emphasized throughout the text, and Caulaincourt seems almost fearful at times when he knows the Emperor is being foolhardy. He describes Napoleon as bad tempered. When he accidentally falls of his horse, "his bad temper and forebodings were obvious despite his efforts at concealment," and he "did all he could to dispel the misgivings which he sensed that everyone must have felt—for men are superstitious despite themselves."[85] When one of his men jumped into the water to save another man, Napoleon felt that such a deed was praiseworthy only in civilian life, but not appropriate "to a colonel at the head of his regiment in the face of the enemy."[86] This is indeed an interesting viewpoint. Although avoiding distractions and remaining at your position in time of war is no doubt important, failing to save a team member would likely weaken rather than strengthen unit cohesion and trust.

Caulaincourt further portrays Napoleon as selfish, driven, lacking compassion, and incompetent due to his refusal to accept the advice given him, even as the men were unable to go on because of the lack of supplies. When informed that men and horses had reached the end of their rope, that the marches were too long and exhausting, the "Emperor paid no attention."[87] According to Caulaincourt, the Emperor was ready to pay any price to reach his objective, and the miserable troops almost wished their horses would die, for it would mean the breakdown of their service and "thus the end to their personal privations," which Caulaincourt considered "the secret and cause of our earlier disasters and of our final reverse."[88] But since the Emperor was unwilling to hear the truth, it had no effect on him. In fact, he was "aggravated with those who had the courage to tell it."[89]

Although Napoleon is portrayed in an exceedingly negative light, one might question whether Caulaincourt displays this image of the Emperor because Caulaincourt was opposed to the war and had asked to be excused from it. Yet the idea that peace was "forever represented by the Emperor as the motive of all his enterprises,"[90] reinforces the notion that a leader can justify his obsession with a goal as long as he can convince his team that it rests on a sound foundation (in this case, peace). Is there a risk that a passionate leader might lead his team down the wrong trench?

THE ALLURING FORMULA OF WAR

As demonstrated through the previous examples, one can no doubt be enlightened by viewing leadership through a military prism. War is a profoundly human experience and as such is guided by human emotions and passion. But would those who have fought on our battlefields really recommend war as a classroom for learning team leadership in the civilian workplace? Do civilian businessmen and women and military personnel really understand each other? What problems might one face as a result of a desire to Lead with War?

Although it is tempting to draw parallels between combat leadership and civilian leadership, the lessons of war are unpredictable and cannot be formed into a list of prescribed solutions to particular problems. According to a handbook about *Infantry in Battle* based on studies of World War experiences, and first prepared under the direction of Colonel George C. Marshall (1880-1959 CE):

> The art of war has no traffic with rules, for the infinitely varied circumstances and conditions of combat never produce exactly the same situation twice . . . It follows, then, that the leader who would become a competent tactician must first close his mind to the alluring formula that well-meaning people offer in the name of victory. To master his difficult art he must learn to cut to the heart of a situation, recognize its decisive elements and base his course of action on these. The ability to do this is not God-given, nor can it be acquired overnight; it is a process of years. He must realize that training in solving problems of all types, long practice in making clear, unequivocal decisions, the habit of concentrating on the question at hand, and an elasticity of mind, are indispensable requisites for the successful practice of the art of war. The leader who frantically strives to remember what someone else did in some slightly similar situation has

already set his feet on a well-traveled road to ruin.[91]

The above paragraph offers food for thought for the aspiring and field-tested leader alike: Leadership is comprised of "infinitely varied circumstances" . . . it "never produce[s] exactly the same situation twice" . . . one must "close [one's] mind to the alluring formula that well-meaning people offer" . . . leadership is "not God-given" and cannot "be acquired overnight; it is a process of years." (Are leaders born or made?) What does this tell us? It suggests that those pursuing leadership in earnest might be wise to avoid trampling the path prescribed by well-meaning but gung-ho men and women who spend their days dreaming up all sorts of bumper sticker slogans which, although possibly proving motivational for a day, lack substance in the real world.

Carl von Clausewitz (1780-1831 CE), an early nineteenth century Prussian soldier and military theorist, concluded that although victory in combat lies in the planning, determining truth or falsehood at any particular moment often proves to be a gamble and chance, an inherent element of war, tends to sabotage the best-laid plans.[92] A talented leader can hope for a strong position in the world only when his character and familiarity with leadership fortify each other, and only when he obeys his own principles which result from his own judgment. But he cannot necessarily expect a subordinate to embrace those same principles, unless the subordinate has come to his own conclusion that the principles are sound. Theory, thus, should aid judgment but not tell one what to do.

Certainly not all agree. Some military leaders believe that leadership can in fact be calculated according to an alluring formula. Antoine-Henri Jomini (1779-1869 CE), a French general serving under the celebrated war hero Napoleon Bonaparte and perhaps the most significant writer of the Napoleonic Wars of the early nineteenth century, viewed leadership as a science, not an art, and would have disagreed with the statement that leadership in combat is comprised of "infinitely varied circumstances." Jomini perceived warfare in heroic terms and believed that Napoleon's successes could directly be attributed to his adherence to a select number of scientifically determined principles, and his failures to a neglect of adherence to the same.

According to Jomini, military action consists of weapons and techniques as well as political and moral factors. Tactics are determined by the kinds of weaponry used. But only strategy, because of its unchanging nature, can undergo scientific analysis. He thus attempted to prescribe how to make strategic choices intended to "reduce the problem of war to the professional concerns of the wartime commander."[93] He preferred the type of warfare that relied on a mutual agreement between enemies to do battle (in other words, the predictable type), and not on the type that relied on the general population murdering "isolated soldiers,"[94] as he described it. This preference might account for his attempts to reduce warfare and leadership to a precise science. Take a moment and ponder the following statement:

> The question has often been discussed, whether it is preferable to assign to the command a general of long experience in service with troops, or an officer of the staff, having generally but little experience in the management of troops. It is beyond question that war is a distinct science of itself, and that it is quite possible to be able to combine operations skillfully without ever having led a regiment against an enemy. Peter the Great, Condé, Frederick, and Napoleon are instances of it. It cannot, then, be denied that an officer from the staff may as well as any other prove to be a great general, but it will not be because he has grown gray in the duties of a quartermaster that he will be capable of the supreme command, but because he has a natural genius for war and possesses the requisite characteristics.[95]

Jomini suggested that since war is a "distinct science," success does not rely so much on direct experience as on an ability to use theoretical knowledge and calculations. Thus an officer from the staff who has never led a regiment against an enemy may prove to be a great general, particularly if he has a "natural genius," an inborn talent, for war. (Again, are leaders born or made?) Jomini further believed that the scientific approach to war would allow one to create a checklist for action, which could be marked off successfully without considering such factors as human nature, chance, and other uncertainties that might develop during the course of a campaign. He also tended to overlook the possibility of failure. Not only did he select the specific campaigns that best suited his purpose, he failed to follow sound scientific doctrine. In other words, he failed to test the "historical cases in which actual military experience did not conform to prediction based on his principles."[96] While he focused only on the military commanders and their interests—his close proximity to Napoleon and Marshal Ney probably influenced his ambitions—he was vague about "where the principles of war do and do not apply."[97] Sometimes victory depended on adherence to the principles; other times on the military commander.

What we can learn from this is that when the outcome of an act conforms to predictions, it is easy to fall into the trap of believing that the principle used to achieve success will hold true in all situations. However, the analytically driven leader will examine also those cases where the particular principle failed to achieve success. A comparison can be drawn to many modern leadership studies, which likewise tend to rely on the list-type approach, or cookbook for success, as I like to call it. A few examples include: *The 21 Irrefutable Laws of Leadership* by John C. Maxwell and Stephen R. Covey; *The One Minute Manger* by Kenneth H. Blanchard and Spencer Johnson; *Monday Morning Leadership: Eight Mentoring Sessions You Cannot Afford to Miss* by David Cottrell; *The Five Dysfunctions of a Team* by Patrick Lencioni; *The Leadership Moment: Nine Stories of Triumph and Disaster and Their Lessons for Us All* by Michael Useem and Warren Bennis; and *Quiet Leadership: Six Steps to Transforming Performance at Work* by David Rock. Note how each of the aforementioned studies relies on a checklist (Eight Mentoring Sessions, Nine Stories, Six Steps, etc.) that one can memorize and that implies that, if followed, success is more or less guaranteed.

In their book, *The Five Practices of Exemplary Leadership*, authors Jim Kouzes and Barry Posner identify five practices that, if followed, are intended to help leaders get their team to perform extraordinary things. The five practices are: Challenging the Process; Inspiring a Shared Vision; Enabling Others to Act; Modeling the Way; and Encouraging the Heart. It is difficult to criticize the effect that these principles correctly executed would have on the team. Yet their general nature is precisely the reason why it is difficult to disagree, and also why it is difficult to disagree with famous military strategists such as Sun-tzu who have a tendency to state the obvious. The difficulty, of course, lies not in stating the obvious but in bringing the obvious to action.

So who was correct: Carl von Clausewitz in his assertion that, "[e]xperience is of more value in the Art of War than all philosophical truth,"[98] or Jomini in his belief that it is "possible to be able to combine operations skillfully without ever having led a regiment against an enemy"? Regardless of which stand you take, a danger with the checklist approach (or cookbook for success), and with reducing a profoundly human activity such as war and/or leadership to a science, is that it provides a means for avoiding critical thinking. We will examine this issue in greater detail in Parts II and III of this book: Leading with Cheese, Fish, and Carrots; and Leading with Science.

WHAT ABOUT THE GREAT MEN?

Military history—written by generals, military theorists, historians, revolutionaries, and emperors and kings—has been explored, picked apart, hammered out, examined, categorized, and put back together again. Political and military analysts, proponents and opponents of different theories of war, have used history in attempts to improve battlefield tactics and strategy; to inspire generals and foot soldiers standing at the threshold of armed conflict; and to justify society's position, its "righteousness" to clash with the enemy. The sources we study influence how history is written, but how history is written also influences the availability of the sources. After examining what is on the shelves in bookstores, can we not say the same about leadership studies?

What is the structure of the discipline? We probably agree that leadership is a series of events that were experienced at some point by the author, and that the author believes he or she has an important message to pass on to future generations; in other words, wisdom that future leaders can use according to their own needs, times, and circumstances. No doubt do political and cultural beliefs, as well as personal desires and biases—in short, the needs of the writers and the needs of the users of leadership—influence the literature of the discipline. Objective interpretation of events is therefore difficult to achieve, and one person's views or experiences may not give us enough practical insight to properly instruct or inspire others. Just as the historian understands that the expressions and intents of the narratives rest with the creators of the works, so must the scholar of leadership understand the importance of examining the sources of the written works. From what point of view do the writers write? What are their educations and backgrounds? What cultural beliefs influence their ideas? Do they draw their knowledge from other sources or are they eyewitnesses to the events they describe? Perhaps most importantly: What are their motivations for writing a particular narrative, and for whom do they write?

Those who are fond of Leading with War and using historical sources of Great Men who, through their character, insight, or compassion have managed to inspire generations of business executives, civilian leaders, and armchair warriors would be wise to remember that historical ideas of the past are seldom timeless, because they can seldom be duplicated and transported to another era flawlessly. The popular view of history at the time the narrative is written is therefore an important issue for consideration, especially if we intend to use the account for instructional purposes at a later date.

Furthermore, our biases and tendencies to turn a blind eye to that which we find disagreeable becomes evident if we do but the briefest examination of the Great Men who have made an impact on history. Sun-tzu in the East and Napoleon Bonaparte in the West are two of the most influential strategic thinkers, despite the fact that Napoleon failed to write detailed accounts of his own campaigns. In America, Civil War General Robert E. Lee undoubtedly takes the lead. By contrast, Adolf Hitler, who theorized about a perfect world, is so despised (justly so, since he was a mass murderer) that we tend to take the greatest care to avoid everything he said, no matter how insightful it might have been. Why? Because war history is often political in nature, and the proponents of a particular view influence the degree to which this view is spread and cross-utilized in other disciplines such as leadership. But surely even Adolf Hitler, Karl Marx, and Mao Zedong had a valuable insight or two to share with us current and future generation leaders? Would you not nod in agreement at the following statements, at least until you learn who said what?

1. We think too small, like the frog at the bottom of the well. He thinks the sky is only as big as the top of the well. If he surfaced, he would have an entirely different view.

2. Reason has always existed, but not always in a reasonable form.

3. Words build bridges into unexplored regions.

Statement number 1 above is attributed to Mao Zedong; number 2 to Karl Marx; and number 3 to Adolf Hitler. I fully expect to take heat or stir controversy with my suggestion that we should acknowledge the insights of our enemies or opposition, even those who we despise the most. But bear in mind that the point of this exercise is not to justify any particular political view or human atrocity, but to demonstrate how we form biases based on the political and cultural influences in our lives. Good leaders need broad horizons, which is all the more reason to develop critical thinking skills, discuss unpleasant facts, and avoid falling in lockstep with the many popular slogans that are so frequently recited in books and at leadership seminars. Although motivational writers and speakers frequently display good advice, it can be misleading if taken out of context or placed in the wrong time or circumstance. When we Lead with War and promote the leadership principles of the great historical generals, we also fall into the trap of using historical examples to justify a belief or viewpoint, or what we perceive to be true as seen from our particular position.

There are, of course, inherent difficulties associated with determining the validity and, therefore, the usefulness of a particular viewpoint. In war, is the foot soldier more correct in his views than the commanding officer, or than the TV viewers for that matter, who experience the war from the safety of their living rooms? In civilian leadership, is the employee more correct in his views than the supervisor or manager, or the customers for that matter, who have an entirely different set of concerns? Or is the commanding officer or the supervisor the higher authority?

In addition to written accounts of war, popular history also includes expressions that grow out of military conflict, for example, *Blitzkrieg*. In contemporary times, expressions such as shock and awe, winning hearts and minds, mother of all wars, and smoke them out of their holes, come to mind. Popular expressions in civilian leadership include, always room for improvement, half-full is better than half-empty, abandon four-letter words, and there is no "I" in team. These slogans are full of limitations because the needs of the writers and the needs of the users of leadership (the leaders as well as the followers) differ, and the viewpoints and expressions are essentially as numerous as the writers.

Those who desire to Lead with War and choose to study the Great Men of history should be wary of the fact that Great Men can be categorized into different groups depending on their primary objectives. The first category includes those who write for the purpose of developing war strategy to teach and motivate the recruits in the military academies who read the works. These writers might make inferences between ancient accounts of battles and future war strategies. The second category includes those who are (or were) mere observers of war, for example, the *skalds* (court poets) who accompanied the Norse kings on campaign specifically with the intent of recording what happened and relating it later, usually in verse. The skald had a tough job: Although it was his duty to praise the king, he would lose credibility if he spoke any untruths. Thus if the king were defeated in battle, the skald was left with the difficult task of speaking the truth while still honoring the king with praise of heroism. The third category includes those who have distinguished themselves on campaign and write for the purpose of recording their own greatness, as might be the case, for example, with Julius Caesar, whose "military genius" has been studied and quoted widely. But one wonders, too, what Caesar's motives were when writing the *Commentaries*. Since he was a gifted speaker and writer who employed a sophisticated rhetoric, it is possible that he wrote foremost because he enjoyed listening to his own discourse. The fourth category includes the foot soldiers, or those who have experienced the war firsthand from the most disadvantaged positions. Again, the needs of the writers and the needs of the users of history differ. If leadership books were written primarily by the "foot soldiers" or the employees of civilian corporations, who are subjected to all kinds of leadership principles, would such books as *Who Moved My Cheese?* by Spencer Johnson and Kenneth Blanchard really reach the bestseller list?

Our search for knowledge binds us to the goals, desires, and individual interpretations of the historians. Whether we study warfare for military purposes or for the education of civilians, the stories of particular wars and Great Men are certainly welcome because they help us identify with our past, search for logical links between past and present or future, and drive home points. But they are not necessarily indicative of how we ought to proceed within our own organization which is often thousands of miles and centuries removed from the event in question.

THE OBVIOUS AND THE NOT SO

While it is tempting to draw parallels between the past and the present, the reasoning we use is not always accurate. The successes and failures of Great Men such as Sun-tzu, Napoleon, and Robert E. Lee can be attributed at least in part to the particular circumstances of their day. Robert E. Lee, for example, faced the daunting task of defending an extensive territory without adequate means, and struggled with the question of whether to invade the North or stay in the South and defend against Union assaults. He reasoned that an offensive-defensive strategy would allow the Confederacy to take the initiative and, after having determined the critical points, muster the forces to attack these points successfully despite the South's inferior strength. He enlisted the help of Stonewall Jackson (1824-1863 CE), who had a reputation for exploiting the enemy by using superior intelligence measures when outnumbered. However, due to his limited manpower resources, Lee's offensive strategy proved questionable at best.

The Confederacy's system of coastal defense also proved inefficient, because the advent of modern guns and the steam engine gave ships greater maneuverability than in the past; an asset that the enemy could use to their advantage when protecting themselves against fire. A combination of Union blockades, amphibious coastal assaults, control of the Mississippi, and almost uninterrupted tries to capture the southern capital further deprived the Confederacy of much needed supplies and weakened Lee's army.[99] The Confederacy erred because it attempted to wage warfare by using old battlefield concepts in combination with new innovations in weaponry. Although Lee displayed good leadership qualities, relied on cunning advisers, and was truly beloved by his men, the firing technology of the time proved superior to these factors and wiped out large parts of his army. The war naturally took a turn toward attrition and the eventual defeat of the Confederacy.

Sun-tzu faced a different problem. While he had a ready answer to every situation the battlefield commander might encounter, much of China's military history revolves around internal conflicts. Sun-tzu's *Art of War* thus assumes a Chinese opponent and pays little attention to the problems associated with the steppe people and other mounted warriors. It pays even less attention to the skills that a civilian man or woman born into the Western world two and a half millennia later might need to master leadership problems that occur within his or her particular office or organization.

So why do we continue to promote Sun-tzu's *Art of War* as a leadership book for the modern businessman and woman? One reason is because leaders tend to see what they wish to see, and are more accepting of evidence that supports their particular viewpoint than of evidence that challenges it. We tend to find connections between events because we have on our minds those things that we are searching for, while overlooking others. The Chinese texts prove popular because they allow for a broad array of interpretations and can easily be cherry-picked by Western businessmen as they see fit. Saying, "yes, that is true," or "yes, of course, that makes sense," reinforces beliefs that we may already hold, simultaneously allowing us to turn a blind eye to that which is unpleasant.

But any military or civilian leadership model requires an intellectual pursuit that exceeds this "cookbook for success" approach. Those who plaster their walls with isolated sayings and slogans, which are often displayed out of context from the situations in which they first occurred, will not realize true success beyond a temporary "feel good" moment. Although Great Men who have performed admirably in warfare sort of give us a free license to use their stories of heroic struggles as motivation for current and future leaders, we also have a great capacity to misuse much of what history has supposedly taught us. Yes, the leader's job in the workplace is to get the workers to accomplish certain tasks, generally with speed and efficiency. But as one of my professors in military history school taught me, although a checklist may be a good servant, it is not necessarily a good master.[100]

So if not through the checklist, how do you move people to action? Popular passion is necessary, of course, particularly when personal sacrifice is needed. Ancient Greece which is credited with giving birth to democracy or the "rule of many," as defined by

Aristotle (384-322 BCE), was hostile to ancient Rome, so naturally many battles were fought. All male citizens were expected to participate in warfare. But in contrast to fighting for the ambitions of a king or dictator, they had a stake in the outcome; they fought for personal freedom and the security of their family, farm, and civilian lifestyle. Defending these ideals paid off on personal terms. If there is no payoff, the leader (or king or dictator or boss) is merely engaging in self-serving interests and cannot expect the team to follow willingly. Sometimes the leader's job is to create popular passion and motivate the team to accept a change that in the leader's mind will lead to greater results; or as is so often stated, to work smarter but not harder. But why should the team want to work smarter? What is the payoff?

In my youth I delivered mail for the post office. It was the best job I have ever had. Each letter carrier was responsible for sorting and delivering the mail to the recipients who lived within his or her district. Whether you worked fast or slow, you still received the same pay for delivering the day's mail to your district. Thus if you could finish the job in three rather than eight hours by working smarter, as frequently happened, you could take the rest of the day off with full pay. It was a win-win for everybody. The customers were happy because they received their mail in the morning instead of the afternoon; the postal workers were happy because they could go home several hours early each day and still get paid as if they had worked eight hours; and the boss was happy because of the many letters and phone calls of praise he received from the customers for the good service. On the other hand, had he reduced the workforce and awarded fewer breaks as "thanks" for the effort, the workers would inevitably have been less eager to work "smarter."

"Progress is made by lazy men looking for easier ways to do things," suggests science fiction writer Robert Heinlein (1907-1988 CE).[101] If you reward the team for working smarter with longer breaks, or perhaps even allow them to go home early with full pay, they will inevitably find a way to work smarter. The ancient Chinese military classic, *T'ai Kung's Six Secret Teachings*, states that in general, "in employing rewards one values credibility; in employing punishments one values certainty. When rewards are trusted and punishments inevitable wherever the eye sees and the ear hears, then even where they do not see or hear there is no one who will not be transformed in their secrecy."[102] The ancient Greek historian and soldier Xenophon likewise reminded us that, "[t]he sweetest of all sounds is praise," and, "[m]en who think that their officer recognizes them are keener to be seen doing something honorable and more desirous of avoiding disgrace."[103] But keep in mind that while rewarding good behavior is honorable, doing nothing when punishment is called for is as bad as being too lenient or too harsh, because by doing nothing, you are in effect failing to reinforce good behavior while giving quiet approval of bad behavior. By failing to punish bad behavior, you are in effect punishing the good workers for their good behavior. If this is the case, then why would any worker want to work smarter? This is so obvious it should go without saying. However, if left unstated, it can with time be forgotten.

What is not obvious? Although you have probably told your team at some point that if it ain't broke there is still room for improvement and half-full is better than half-empty, it is not obvious that it is really so. It is also not obvious that others think like you and like what you think; that there is no "I" in team and together everybody achieves more; or, as Napoleon would have us believe, that secondary matters will settle themselves. If Leading with War is your preferred leadership style, you might want to take to heart the observations of American journalist Robert D. Kaplan: Although "[t]he Army Reserve is desperate for officers . . . there is little urge among American elites to volunteer."[104] What this statement implies is that our leaders are not very eager to sacrifice for their team and cause, even as they are mouthing off about honor and heroism and service to God and country. What do you owe your team, and what does your team owe you outside of what is stated in your written contract? Or do you owe each other nothing but eight hours of work and a paycheck? We will explore these questions in more detail in Part III of this book.

HISTORY DOES NOT REPEAT ITSELF

Whether you are a true military man or woman or an armchair warrior who spend your weekends dreaming about leading a group of motivated and talented individuals into battle and emerging a celebrated hero, as evidenced by the difficulty associated with defining it in a single sentence, leadership is not the proprietary domain of a select group of people. One thing that should be learned from war history, or any history for that matter, is that contrary to popular belief history does NOT repeat itself.

History consists of a long row of less than pleasant events. But what sets humans apart from animals is our ability to learn from the accumulated knowledge of those who went before us. Yet when you have worked for a company for twenty years, you have no doubt been through the same cycle of mistakes several times under different leadership, or even more frightening, under the same leadership. As has been said, "Throw a man in the river, and as soon as his clothes have dried, he shall be the same as before." So if history does not repeat itself, then why the same cycle of mistakes? Why do we not learn from the past? As expressed quite eloquently by the ancient Greek philosopher Heraclitus (c. 535-475 BCE), one reason why is because, "[n]o man ever steps in the same river twice, for it is not the same river and he is not the same man."[105]

Historical "cultures" are rarely interchangeable. Take the following example: In 2003 Delta Air Lines created a wholly owned subsidiary called Song Airlines and based it on Southwest Airlines' leadership model: No frills, no first class, no free meals, and quick turnaround time of flights. Song Airlines became an "invitation for a lifestyle."[106] The company advertised for "talent leaders" instead of "team leaders." Song Airlines folded after barely three years of service. Why? Because, contrary to popular belief, history does NOT repeat itself, and when the borrower of an idea fails to heed its own company's history the adopted "culture" is likely to fail.

We tend to reason by false analogy and draw information from familiar situations of the past in an attempt to relate these to unfamiliar situations of today. But this works only if the past and the present are truly the same and not just appearing similar. Thus while it is tempting to use historical examples as guidelines for future strategy, we should remember that history, as it happens, lacks the benefit of hindsight, and whether a choice is wise or not must often be determined at a later date. We can always look back and say that a particular principle was sound, but we cannot look forward with the same confidence. If Song Airlines had succeeded, we would look back and say that Delta Air Lines made a wise choice. But since we have to rely on hindsight whenever we make a decision for change, and Song Airlines had no history when it was created, we cannot say in advance whether or not our choice will be wise. History might be able to tell us what not to do, but it can rarely tell us what to do. This is one reason why it is difficult to use books such as Sun-tzu's *Art of War* as prescriptions for future strategy. Or as military strategist Carl von Clausewitz reminded us, "[S]kill already developed may be refined by the study of past examples, but skill is only acquired in actually dealing with present examples."[107]

Clausewitz's insights were profound. Although he concluded that historical examples could be used in four ways: to "explain an idea; to demonstrate the application of an idea; to support a statement and so show that a phenomenon was possible; and to give a detailed account of a historical event in order to deduce a doctrine,"[108] he did not suggest that another person's story had universal utility or could be used as an unbiased source that would ultimately lead to success:

> Although using history as a critic and theorist rather than as a historian, Clausewitz was sufficiently historically minded to be aware of the difficulties which sources pose for historians. Equipped with hindsight, they could see things much more clearly than could the commander on the ground, and those who were not practitioners fell back on empty phrases which sounded expert but conveyed little. Reading a general's memoirs was not likely to be much more helpful, because they tended to be selective and self-serving.[109]

Writers of leadership books frequently try to import the concept but not the culture. But if the concept springs from the culture, to truly have a full importation of the concept, the culture must be imported too. Thus if you borrow the military leadership theories of say the Rogue Warrior Richard Marcinko, you must also borrow the rest of the culture upon which his theories are founded. For instance, the Rogue Warrior suggests as one of his Ten Commandments of SpecWar (Special Warfare or Special Operations Forces) that with respect to the team you treat "all alike—just like shit."[110] Would this work within your organization? What do you say, should you treat everyone the same or differently? Should you treat everyone poorly (like shit) until they have proven themselves to you? People are individuals and, although the employees who work under you may be a team, it is their individualism that gives the team its strength. Moreover, individuals react differently to the same treatment. While rough treatment may help some, it will destroy others. How about this: "If you are not tough enough to take a little criticism, you should not be in this position," or, "What does not kill you makes you stronger." Good or bad?

If there is still confusion as to why history appears to repeat itself, consider for a moment the insights of Renaissance Italian political philosopher and Florentine statesman Niccolo Machiavelli: "[W]ise men say, and not without reason, that whoever wishes to foresee the future must consult the past; for human events ever resemble those of preceding times"?[111] However, as Machiavelli further explains, the reason why this is so is because men and women of our time are motivated by the same passions as men and women of the past. We therefore let passion rule over reason and frequently repeat mistakes that seem frighteningly similar to those made by generations long gone. This is not the same as saying that we can use examples from the past to build detailed strategies for future success. Moreover, the job of the historian is not merely to state the facts or describe what happened (anybody can do that; it requires only rote memorization), but to bring new views to old events. In concept, this idea can be related to writing poetry or music lyrics. In how many ways can you talk about love or pain, for example? While the old cliché, "there is nothing new under the sun," has continuity, what one acquires is often a result of what one is searching for. New combinations of the old can give the appearance of originality even though there is nothing original about them.

Since the study of history involves not only the study of the facts but also the study of the underlying currents that shaped the events, it is always problematic to transfer one's unique interpretation of what happened in the past to current times or to a different craft. Thus the leadership theories of the Rogue Warrior or any other great general apply to the particular military situation they were developed for and not to all situations and times. Although we may learn from the past, we cannot live in it.[112] Examples from the past can sometimes become what we choose to make of them, but they do not truly foreshadow some future event or even make a point. "The British historian A. J. P. Taylor [1906-1990 CE] once said that the only lesson of history is that there are no lessons. Taylor may be right. Looking for past patterns and precedents and applying them to our own time and circumstances is always risky."[113]

Part II

Leading with Cheese, Fish, and Carrots

"Of the best rulers, the people (only) know they exist."

— Lao-tzu

"Few are those who can see with their own eyes and hear with their own hearts."

— Albert Einstein

"The brightest flashes in the world of thought are incomplete, until they have been proved to have their counterparts in the world of fact."

— John Tyndall

WE WOULD RATHER BE RUINED THAN CHANGED

Does leadership have a goal? The purpose of leadership studies is inevitably to achieve victory. The leader can wear different hats. He can lead from the front or the rear; he can present the team with charismatic speeches or follow a model based on Maslow's Hierarchy of Needs. Individual goals further influence how he or she views and writes about the discipline. Proponents of different leadership theories have attempted to inspire current and future leaders without understanding that it is really the followers and not the leaders who need to be inspired, because they alone decide whether or not they will follow. Furthermore, much of what has been written about leadership is noncritical. Although it includes statistics and fancies, it excludes deeper examination and analysis. We accept as presented what we find in books and manuals even as we have no idea to what extent or if it is founded upon sound principles. This leaves us at a crossroads without a standard to guide us. To move a step closer to understanding the relationship between leader and follower, we will now examine, compare, and contrast the tools managers and leaders commonly use when trying to implement new ideas by appealing to the passionate side of the workforce.

When I read Marcus Buckingham's and Curt Coffman's book, *First, Break All the Rules: What the World's Greatest Managers Do Differently*, I thought it the soundest book about leadership ever written. However, I am sorry to report that I cannot say the same for various other "cookbooks" for leadership, ranging from *Who Moved My Cheese? An Amazing Way to Deal with Change in Your Work and in Your Life* by Spencer Johnson and Kenneth Blanchard to *Fish! A Remarkable Way to Boost Morale and Improve Results* by Stephen C. Lundin, et al. Amazing? Hardly. Remarkable? I don't think so. How do we know?

Leadership books and seminars are commonly opened with anecdotal stories for the purpose of engrossing the listener. (Note the opening to the book you are currently reading.) Anecdotes and parables can be viewed as the cornerstones that set the pace for further discussion. A graphic example is *Fish!* which opening paragraph portrays the typical Monday morning attitude: "It was a wet, cold, dark, dreary, dismal Monday in Seattle. . ." Despite the depressing weather and having suffered the recent death of her husband, Mary Jane, the protagonist of the story, has a reputation as a "can do" supervisor. In sharp contrast to Mary Jane's work ethics, however, the "large operations group on the third floor" has become an "unresponsive, unpleasant wasteland." When Mary Jane accepts a promotion to manager, she suddenly sees the "light" and realizes that "we choose our attitude."[114] Wow! What a revelation! The trick and, subsequently, the gist of the story is how to teach this insight to the "unpleasant wasteland" on the third floor.

Another graphic example is *Who Moved My Cheese?* which provides a parable portraying two mice in search of cheese. (Cheese, in this case, symbolizes that which one treasures, normally one's current job because it is also one's livelihood.) The purpose of the story is to demonstrate how to deal with unwanted change by "moving with the cheese," or not letting the loss of your job (and your livelihood) dictate how you feel about your future. "But, have you noticed how we don't want to change when things change?"[115] asks one character in the story, thus setting the pace for the inevitable change that will follow. It is suggested that rather than stewing about the loss of your job, you should pick up your virtual running shoes and chase after new "cheese" (a new career). By doing so you acknowledge that how you ultimately deal with change has nothing to do with external factors, such as corporate greed or an economic depression, but can be boiled down to your attitude which is the root of all your problems. In my view, adopting a positive attitude is a superficial and overly simplistic solution to dealing with change. Real problems, such as the loss of one's job and livelihood, require real solutions and not just a "good attitude."

However, a reason why these sorts of books are so popular, or even needed, is because the authors realize that employees naturally resist change, and that management will face a barrier every time they are the carriers of bad news such as job cuts, pay cuts, or reorganization where employees are negatively affected and forced into new positions or new duties. But good leadership, although a complex issue, ain't rocket science, and the reliance on anecdotes and metaphors for success can backfire by making the readers of such books feel underappreciated, or worse, insulted and manipulated as evidenced by the volume of less than flattering reviews on Amazon.com for *Fish!* and particularly for *Who Moved My Cheese?*

What do these reviews say? A few examples include "corporate brainwashing" for managers who believe in change for change's sake; and patronizing, shallow, and insulting to the reader's intelligence. The message of *Who Moved My Cheese?* is that "you must not struggle" and must "accept change without regard to whether it is appropriate or not," says one reviewer. The book is clearly written for those with power to be presented to those without power. "It is little wonder that managers, CEOs, teachers, and pretty much anyone with authority over others praise this book," says another reviewer and suggests that the book is "used as a tool by management to cow their herds into submission." Remember how the ancient Greek historian Thucydides reminded us that the natural law of humanity is that the weaker are subject to the stronger, and those who are stronger can naturally use their strength to force their subjects into compliance. Thus the strong do what they can and the weak suffer what they must. The "moral of the story," says one reviewer, "is that we should not get angry when our life bread is constantly moved and hidden from us by some invisible higher power. Instead, we should not only embrace the fact [that] we are being messed with, but also have FUN with it."

Although it may appear as though I am unfairly picking on this particular book, the reason why is because it turned out to be such a tremendous bestseller and thus a book that many of the readers will likely be familiar with. To be fair, it should be mentioned that the book has received just as many positive reviews, but the number of one-star reviews at nearly five hundred is still overwhelming and sends a clear message about how employees come to distrust management when they feel they are being manipulated.

Who Moved My Cheese? can thus be used as a tool by management in lieu of direct communication when major and unpleasant changes in the form of layoffs and pay cuts are on the horizon. I am not alone in this assessment. Barbara Ehrenreich, social critic, journalist, and author of *Bright-Sided: How the Relentless Promotion of Positive Thinking Has Undermined America*, notes how "the promoters of positive thinking present those with a negative attitude, even when it comes to lay-offs and deep pay cuts, as 'whiners.'"[116] She goes on to say:

> The motivation industry could not repair this new reality. All it could do was offer to change how one thought about it, insisting that corporate restructuring was an exhilaratingly progressive "change" to be embraced, that job loss presented an opportunity for self-transformation, that a new batch of "winners" would emerge from the turmoil. And this is what corporations were paying the motivation industry to do. As the *Washington Post* reported in a 1994 article on motivational products, "Large corporations are looking for innovative and cheap ways to boost employees demoralized by massive layoffs." [In the 1990s], AT&T sent its San Francisco staff to a big-tent motivational event called "Success 1994" on the same day the company announced that it would lay off fifteen thousand workers in the coming two years.[117]

The two mice in *Who Moved My Cheese?* try to keep life simple by avoiding analysis and debate. (Remember that debate tends to make things complicated, as suggested by Chinese statesman and military leader Deng Xiaoping.) This is a classic example of what is wrong with seeing the glass as half-full rather than half-empty for fear of being called a whiner. Change, management suggests, is merely a steppingstone to success, and a layoff is really just an opportunity to start that new career you always wanted, no matter the fact that you will not be able to pay your mortgage or feed your family while you are scurrying around in the labyrinth in search of new cheese. In my view, a better approach, as Ehrenreich points out, is to "acquire the skills not of positive thinking but of critical thinking, and critical thinking is inherently skeptical. The best students—and in good colleges, also the most successful—are the ones who raise sharp questions, even at the risk of making a professor momentarily uncomfortable."[118]

Who Moved My Cheese? will no doubt prove suitable for leaders discussing with other leaders what leadership ought to be, but with no interest in involving the subordinates in the decision-making process. Moreover, success through positive thinking has limits. Although the adage, "Move with the cheese!" might reinforce what one already believes, it will unlikely have lasting value or cause an about-face with respect to a situation that has already gone bad. A good leader must commit himself or herself to studying leadership with a critical eye. Here the authors fail to think the thought to conclusion; they fail to ask the appropriate questions and fail to restate the problem from the perspective of the opposition in a way that is satisfactory to the readership. Believing that you can teach people to like change, or stop "hemming and hawing" and "just move with the cheese," suggests either careless or arrogant thinking.

Implementing drastic change when faced with a global economic depression is one thing. But some leaders, supervisors, or managers try to implement change even when change is not needed and the system ain't broke to begin with. Why? Sometimes it is to further their own interests. They know that if they can present a list of "improvements" to their managers or the company, they have a greater chance of being promoted. They can then leave their current position for some higher assignment elsewhere and leave the disgruntled employees to deal with these "improvements" that were not welcome to begin with and did not create greater efficiency. Employees are more willing to change when they recognize that there is an advantage to changing. Before asking people to change, the intelligent and critical leader makes an absolutely honest assessment of his or her true reason for desiring change, and asks if the change will truly bring improvement. He must also be willing to live the change. If his sole motivation is a promotion, the fact that he is dishonest will quickly come to light and sabotage the respect his employees have previously afforded him.

In contrast to *Who Moved My Cheese?* Marcus Buckingham's and Curt Coffman's book, *First, Break All the Rules*, offers several realistic insights about employee motivation and efficiency at work. Rather than trying to plant the "good vs. bad attitude" idea in the minds of employees who complain about change, the authors suggest that you should accept people as they are by recognizing that people have feelings and are naturally resistant to change. The best you can do is avoid generalizations and "[f]ocus on each person's strengths and manage around his weaknesses."[119] In other words, if you have to announce job or pay cuts, accept the fact that your announcement will be received with a great deal of negativity. Then solicit ideas from employees that may make the change less painful and, whenever possible, avoid forcing people into positions they are not interested in. "We would rather be ruined than changed, we would rather die in our dread than climb the cross of the moment and let our illusions die," said British-born American poet Wystan Hugh Auden (1907-1973 CE).[120]

ONE MAN'S TREASURE IS ANOTHER MAN'S TRASH

Fish! in my view, is not quite as disturbing as *Who Moved My Cheese?* However, the ideas presented in the book are likewise missing good follow-through. Although there is no doubt that choosing your attitude and having fun at work can provide employees with the capacity to create a more enjoyable work environment and, therefore, more productivity and better relations with customers, the book assumes that we agree on the definition of fun. Yet I can hear the grumbling at my job if the manager were to interrupt in the middle of coffee break (as suggested in the book) and make it mandatory for everyone to cancel whatever plans they might have had for lunch and go to the fish market, because "it is so much fun." The issue has now shifted from, "Let me show you something really fun," to "I am in charge here and decide how you should spend your lunch break." As a result the manager has already alienated at least some of his or her workforce.

If you desire to know your people better, is the fish market necessarily the best place to accomplish this? Perhaps you should invite them to dinner, to your home, on a camping trip, or to a ball game? Any of these ideas may prove satisfactory, but they may also prove disastrous. Furthermore, what should you do with those on your team who do not want to go to whatever outing or activity you have planned? It is, after all, not for you to say whether or not your employees will enjoy spending time with you. Some people enjoy their own company better, or that of their family for that matter. Believe it or not but some people would rather stay at work and work a normal day than spend time in the company of their boss at some picnic or other "fun" event. As an example, one company recently organized a "tour" of sorts in a different city, which purpose it was to show appreciation for the workforce, reinforce the importance of customer service, and promote teamwork by making the employees partake in "friendly" competition. The initial memo that was issued with respect to this idea stated that it was "mandatory" for employees to attend the event, even though it would require spending a night away from home in a shared hotel room with a stranger. When enough people had grumbled, the company thought better of it and made participation voluntary.

When an employee refuses to take part in your suggestions for fun, it does not mean that he or she is inherently a bad worker without social skills, nor does it mean that he or she is not a team player. Although choosing one's attitude and making an attempt to have fun as professed in *Fish!* might indeed create an enjoyable work environment, more productivity, and better customer relations, the same can be said for running a tight ship. When trying to implement new ideas that foster a fun atmosphere at work, you should also not forget to ask what the customer thinks. Say Marcus Buckingham and Curt Coffman about customer service in the airline industry:

> [A]irlines forget that customers don't usually choose one airline over another by comparing safety records. Whatever the airline, customers fully expect that they will arrive at their destination unharmed. They demand safety, but they are not impressed by it. It is the wrong outcome for airlines to emphasize. Southwest Airlines again stands out as the exception. Their flight attendants are experts in all the required safety procedures, but safety is not the point of their work. Fun is the point.[121]

I applaud the authors for their deep insights into successful leadership, but must confess that I disagree on this particular point. To know whether or not the authors are correct, one must first ask the customers who fly Southwest Airlines what they think. It is possible that some customers would find Southwest's leadership model disturbing and would rather have a quiet experience onboard that allows them to read a book or work on their laptop undisturbed. Again, the point is that people's ideas of fun differ. One man's treasure is another man's trash even when it comes to fun. The lesson is: Do not assume. Whether you are dealing with your employees at work or with the customers, make an effort to ask how they really feel. And remember that it is not for you to decide what another person should think is fun.

What tricks in addition to those described previously do companies and motivational writers and speakers use when attempting to motivate employees through the adoption of a "good attitude" and "fun" activities? At one company in briefing one day, the leadership came up with the not so brilliant idea that employees should do a self-evaluation to create peer pressure that would motivate them to work harder and more efficiently, on the premise that work has more meaning when there is a bit of friendly competition involved. If you accomplished a lot in one day you would rate yourself highly on the score card, and if you accomplished a little you would give yourself a lower score. The score cards would then be displayed daily on the bulletin board for all to see. One worker with an outstanding work record raised his hand and asked, "What if we do not want to participate in this exercise?" The leadership answered, "Then you can go home!" Rather than making an effort to learn why this worker was not interested in participating, the leadership punished him merely for asking a question. If you were to take an educated guess, to what extent do you think the leadership managed to motivate this employee?

Here is what happened: After the briefing, the employee went to the leadership's office and expressed dislike of the treatment he had received. He was then somehow suckered into developing the score cards for the exercise. He spent a whole evening at home working on this project without compensation. But when he returned the next day with the score cards, the idea never went into effect. Why? Because by then it had become obvious to the leadership that adults are not going to play games that they have no interest in playing. "When you come up with a bullshit program, you will get bullshit results," the employees told the leadership. But rather than admitting that forcing people to compete who have no interest in competing is not going to increase their motivation, the leadership said that they had never intended to implement the idea in the first place, but wanted only to find out who would approach it with a good attitude and who would not.

If you are in a leadership position and you have an idea for a new program and your people tell you that it will not work, will you listen to them? Or will you tell them that their attitude sucks?

Or perhaps you will use the common excuse that one cannot know whether or not an idea will work before one has tried it? Common sense should tell you differently. Do you like liver? No? Good, I don't either! And, you know, even if I had never tried it, I still would not have the desire to eat it just to find out if I were correct in my assessment of my taste buds. Past experiences along with gut feeling will give a good indication of how efficient a new program or idea is even before one has tried it. Moreover, people are not inherently lazy. Most of us want to work and enjoy contributing with our ideas for the purpose of increasing the efficiency of our organization. Still, what motivates you may be a turnoff to me and vice versa. Thus whether or not games and friendly competition are good motivators is not immediately clear. Motivational ideas cannot be taken at face value just because they are stated in a book that has hit the bestseller list.

GOALS UNDER CONSTRUCTION

Rather than accepting the fact that one man's treasure can be another man's trash, we often try to fit everybody under the same umbrella especially when it comes to motivational ideas. But you cannot change the fact that the world is made up of all kinds of personality types simply because you think you have found this great new way of "transforming" people. As we have seen in the above examples, when management suggests that employees should split into teams and compete for the Holy Grail at the end of the rainbow, the suggestion might backfire because many people are not competitive and therefore not motivated by the idea of competition no matter what the prize. Having fun at work by playing games will only appeal to some of the workers. To take this a step further, consider suggesting to a highly efficient employee that he or she should apply for a supervisor position because "he is so talented," or because "he would be great in the job," or because "people like him need to use their fullest potential," or because "he is wasting his time and talent in his current position." If you are surprised when he refuses your suggestion, it may be because you do not understand that everybody does not value the same things or the same ideas.

Despite its somewhat corny title, Adrian Gostick's and Chester Elton's book, *The Carrot Principle: How the Best Managers Use Recognition to Engage Their Employees, Retain Talent, and Drive Performance*, rises above *Fish!* and *Who Moved My Cheese?* with respect to changing employee attitudes, by emphasizing that "[w]hile leaders cannot often change the tasks in their organization, they can change employees' attitudes toward their jobs by setting clear corporate goals," and "[a] good share of an employee's attitude toward work is internally driven by a person's desire for autonomy and achievement."[122]

Let us return to the overly zealous manager at Bubba's place of employment, who hung miniature hardhats in the door openings to the various offices in an attempt to motivate employees to "construct" new goals. According to Gostick and Elton, "In business, a carrot is something used to inspire and motivate an employee."[123] But the carrot has to be of real value.

Rather than hanging signs reading "Goals Under Construction," this manager might have wanted to start by asking, "Whose goals are under construction?" If the employee's goal does not coincide with management's goal, it is unrealistic to believe that you will reach success with this type of leadership approach. If you have a problem with the current accomplishments of your team, it is better to say so straight out and talk about what can be done (in other words, to call a spade a spade) rather than beating around the bush with sublime messages that act as turnoffs to the greater part of the workforce. Why does every worker have to have a goal, anyway? Face it: Some people work for you only because they need to put food on the table and not because they feel any particular allegiance to your company. If we force people to set goals, many employees will set goals that they have not thought much about rather than goals that lead to something of true value.

Better, Faster, Friendlier, Together = Operational Excellence. "Puff and fluff," said Bubba, then grinned and reached for the thumbtacks and posted the model on the walls in our halls, offices, and break rooms. Cookbook approaches to leadership, such as *The One-Minute Manager* by Kenneth H. Blanchard and Spencer Johnson, or *The 21 Indispensible Qualities of a Leader* by John C. Maxwell, tend to tempt leaders to fall in step with yet another graphic example of a new, efficient, and creative way of doing business. Leaders constantly get trapped in meaningless ideas and sayings that they shamelessly pass on to their followers, sometimes because they proudly believe that it is everybody's responsibility to smile, be proactive, work smarter and not harder, and, above all, that there is no "I" in team, and other times because they know how little thinking power the masses possess. More often, these sorts of leadership approaches offer little new insight. In fact, some of the slogans are so obvious that to mention them in polite company would seem arrogant: "Talent is a Gift, but Character is a Choice."[124] Okay, so what? Not to discuss them, on the other hand, comes with the risk of causing discourse and reality to diverge on separate paths.

Although hundreds of people have offered advice on leadership and leaders are generally fond of using acronyms and analogies when trying to motivate their employees, the phrases and slogans they use are highly imprecise and often rely on what one thinks sounds good at the moment without basing it on factual research. The same ideas and slogans are rehashed over and over without considering their deeper meaning, and are often merely repeats of what other leaders have said or happened to hear at some seminar they attended long ago. In any practical sense, they do not go beyond that first fuzzy feel-good moment and do not explore what happens next. It is also not uncommon for the workers who are exposed to these slogans to avoid questioning their validity, and as a result feel unhappy and dissatisfied with their place of employment when the sayings do not deliver what they promise. To gain proper understanding as an employee you must sometimes be prepared to take the opposite stand and have the moral courage NOT to be politically correct; the courage to dissent openly when management tells you that it is everybody's responsibility and there is no "I" in team. It takes guts to stand up and tell a superior exactly whose responsibility it is (perhaps the janitor's when it comes to cleaning the break room). It takes guts to stand up and tell a superior that he is wrong when suggesting that there is no "I" in team, because the individual—yes "I"—is, in fact, the most important part of a successfully run team.

But how do you know if an idea is valid or not? Consider the following example: You are a motivational speaker teaching a class for supervisors. You tell your audience to clasp their hands and note which thumb overlaps the other. Then you tell them to release their hands and clasp them again. Does the same thumb overlap this time? (Hint: It will for just about everybody.) You now tell your audience that the reason why is because "we have a bad attitude that makes us reluctant to change." The problem with this explanation is that simply holding a demonstration and making a statement does not make it so. What if one person in the audience has the moral courage to speak up and tell you that the reason why the same thumb overlaps the other every time you clasp your hands has more to do with muscle memory and whether you are right or left-handed than with a bad attitude that makes you resistant to change? If you give a right-handed person a pen and asks him or her to write their name on a piece of paper, then ask them to put the pen down, then ask them to pick it up and write their name again, you will find that if they used their right hand the first time they will use it also the second time. You are not going to make a right-handed person more efficient at writing by forcing him or her to use the left hand.

As another example, my friend Bubba's employer forced him to attend a seminar that was teaching what they called "Geometric Psychology," which, in essence, means that you should liken people personalities to different geometric shapes. The square is very organized, writes everything down, and follows the rules by the book. The triangle is the leader and likes to poke his nose into other people's business to see if things are getting done. The circle is the "people person," who gets along great with others and cannot stand spending time alone. The squiggly is the goof, the happy-go-lucky person, who really doesn't worry about much of anything. Bubba compared this idea to palm reading: You find something that fits all people to an extent, and then you tell them what their personality is. In other words, most people will end up having some qualities from each geometric shape. I call it bullshit management. It is a lot of mumbo-jumbo that does not lead anywhere and has no scientific support. The speakers at this seminar further suggested that you should try to change your personality to fit that of the person you are dealing with. I think a better way would be to get to know your people to the extent that you understand their different personalities. If one person in your group tends to get bent out of shape easily yet calms down quickly, by knowing this in advance, you can anticipate his or her behavior without overreacting to it. If one person in your group is exceptionally shy, it is still your responsibility to know him or her so that you can offer help where needed.

Now let us say that you are a somewhat smarter motivational speaker trying to teach your group about change. First you ask everybody to change something in their clothing, such as undoing a necktie, placing their wristwatch on the other arm, or taking a shoe off. Once they have complied, you ask them again to change something in their clothing. Again, they comply. Now, for the third time, you ask that everybody change something in their clothing, but you give no reason for the change. By now you can hear grumbling in the audience. They are beginning to distrust you (the leader). You will now tell the audience that the point of this exercise is to demonstrate that when employees cannot see the benefit of change, they are reluctant to change. You will explain that success is reached by convincing the employees that the change will be beneficial to them. This is pure logic: To convince a person to agree with a conclusion, you must first convince him or her to agree with the premises. If he or she does not agree with the premises, the conclusion will never follow. Yes, you can force change, but if you do your team will not respect you as a leader, they will not stand behind you. You will lose your most important asset: your people. Is it worth it? It has been said that great leaders venture out and find challenges. But keep in mind that the leader cannot exist without the followers and many followers are not interested in challenges that will upset their daily routine. This should be obvious but somehow seems to escape us.

A successful change in attitude must thus be accompanied by clearly defined real change. When sitting in traffic frustrated with the gridlock, rather than thinking of the stop-lights as "go-lights" (as some motivational speakers have suggested), one might opt for leaving home five minutes earlier, choosing an alternate route or, if possible, changing work hours. If you intend to lead with cheese, fish, and carrots, you might want to acknowledge that anecdotal stories and slogans rely on personal conviction rather than hard evidence. Moreover, a person's attitude toward work is largely driven by internal ambitions, and carrot type motivators work only in limited circumstances. According to Daniel H. Pink, author and speechwriter for former Vice President Al Gore:

> For enduring motivation, the science shows, a different approach is more effective. This approach draws not on our biological drive or our reward-and-punishment drive, but on what we might think of as our third drive: Our innate need to direct our own lives, to learn and create new things, and to do better by ourselves and our world.[125]

People are far more likely to change their attitude about a project if they have some ownership of the idea. Ownership is not related to how much money you make, what types of fringe benefits you get, or what kind of uniform you wear. Can you give one specific example of how your team feels ownership? If you were to ask this same question of your team, would they respond with the same example? Remember that a way to test if your ideas have value is to restate them from the perspective of the employees. Is it possible that you believe your team feels ownership of an idea, but when you ask them about it they won't know what you are talking about? As reinforced in *The Carrot Principle*, one of the strongest indicators of employee satisfaction is an opportunity for the employee to do what he or she does best every day.[126]

WINNING HEARTS AND MINDS

Why do we go to work each day? Our jobs are important to us, so important in fact that we go to work even when we hate our jobs. We need the income, but we are also evaluated as people in conjunction with our occupations. What is the first question you ask a new acquaintance? Where do you work? Or, what do you do for a living? Some factors are particularly important in determining how happy we are at work, including permission to decide the specific methods by which we do our job or complete a task. If you have the opportunity to do the things you are good at and enjoy, you will be more likely to come to work with a good attitude, excel, be productive, look for solutions to problems, and less likely to take excessive sick days. This should be obvious. Thus barriers are not necessarily broken by cross-utilizing employees and forcing them to work in areas where they do not want to work. This sort of behavior is more likely to cause discontent, lack of productivity, and more sick days.

Furthermore, how big a part your employees can play in problem solving and how secure they feel at work is directly related to how much information they receive. A common reason for negative reactions toward change is that people feel secure in their present positions and like things "the way they are." Another reason is lack of information about the change. Nobody likes coming to work only to discover that their "map" no longer matches their surroundings. Change should not be implemented solely for the sake of change; however, there are many reasons why a good manager might want to implement change in the workplace. For example, he or she may want to increase the efficiency and quality of the organization and product; new requirements from customers might make change necessary; or some of the current tasks may prove unprofitable and outdated. Something has to be done, but what?

Change can take many directions and a solution that works well for one company may not work equally well for another under similar circumstances. Conceptually, however, there are certain stages of change that can act as guidelines and which make your employees feel that their opinions count:

1. **Planning.** This involves selecting representatives from the different departments that the change will affect, who will then brainstorm for the best way to implement the change. When brainstorming, as we will see later, the task is not to come up with as many suggestions as possible, but to come up with the fewest number of truly good suggestions.

2. **Mapping.** Problems can be targeted and diagnosed through discussions in small groups or one-on-one between management and the employees. A list of issues to be discussed will keep the session on track. Remember to talk about both good and bad points; things that already function well and things that need to be remedied. Otherwise the positive things that do not need to be changed may be overlooked in the strife for change, and the end result may be change for the sake of change but without really making things "better."

3. **Implementation.** Before a change can be implemented, it must be considered in view of the ideas that emerged during discussion and brainstorming sessions. During the implementation stage of the change, those affected must get the full support of management, and management must be open to further suggestions for fine-tuning the change.

4. **Evaluation.** An honest evaluation a few weeks and again a few months after the change has been implemented will help guard against employee and customer dissatisfaction. If the change did not accomplish the desired results, more fine-tuning needs to be done with employee input openly talked about and valued.

As has been demonstrated, before implementing new ideas the leader must first win the hearts and minds of his people. Successful leadership requires insight into human personality, which cannot be summarized in a simple saying posted on your office door. No matter how great the idea is, unless others feel ownership they are not likely to support you. Just ask yourself whose ideas you like the most: those that you come up with yourself or those that somebody else comes up with? Generally we like our own idea the best regardless of whether or not it is really the best idea. Even though it is difficult to achieve your best by keeping things the same, you must consider how change affects others. Employees will more readily accept change if the idea originates with them and not with the supervisor or manager. If the leader wants his people to accept change, he must be ready to listen to and implement changes suggested by the employees.

PASSING THE BUCK

But what if one of your employees suggests a change that you agree with, but you have to push it past the higher managers in the chain of command and get approval before you can implement it? Are you willing to do this? At one company, although the supervisor often said that he agreed with the workers, he still passed the buck: "I hear you and I agree, but management doesn't want us to do that!" Sometimes the team leader or boss tries to distance himself from the matter by transferring responsibility to the team through such jargon as, "it has come to my attention . . ." instead of "I have noticed . . ." or "safety is everybody's responsibility," instead of "I am responsible for your safety," or "to tell you the truth," instead of "I don't know but will find out," or the dreaded "you know what I mean?" which effectively bars all further questioning.

Going through the chain of command is often a terrible sacrifice of time and effort and your needs will likely get lost in the bureaucracy. A chain also tends to break at its weakest link. If the chain breaks, you will get no further than to the broken link.

> There was only one catch and that was Catch-22, which specified that a concern for one's own safety in the face of dangers that were real and immediate was the process of a rational mind. Orr was crazy and could be grounded. All he had to do was ask; and as soon as he did, he would no longer be crazy and would have to fly more missions. Orr would be crazy to fly more missions and sane if he didn't, but if he was sane he had to fly them. If he flew them he was crazy and didn't have to; but if he didn't want to he was sane and had to.[127]

The Catch-22 is that to get anything done you must go through the chain of command, because only the top has the authority to do something. But the closer you are to the bottom, the less important the matter will seem to the top. Those who can do something about the matter have the least interest in doing anything. But to get anything done, you must enlist the people who are the least interested in doing something.

Some leeway with principles will always work to your benefit. Managers who try to lead the employees from behind a desk in an office located at headquarters many miles away will make faulty assumptions. Things can look great in theory or on the drawing board, but when you enter the trenches (for those who like to Lead with War), events will not come down exactly the way you thought. After all, your employees do have brains. Even worse is to preach one thing and do another. When you set contradictory rules from behind a desk, as soon as you leave the office and enter the real world where things happen, you will discover that it is impossible to follow all rules as stated. You will therefore break some rules to "facilitate efficiency," or whatever statement you choose to justify your behavior. Your team will not view your behavior kindly unless you also extend the same flexibility to them.

Let us say that your employees complain about the work schedule and you recognize that ownership is important to motivation. So you tell them to delegate one person on the team as the "scheduling agent," who will be responsible for constructing a work schedule that everybody is reasonably happy with. You might have been against this idea at first but feel relieved on second thought, because now you have more free time on your hands which allows you to disappear to the coffee shop. When the work load suddenly gets heavy, the scheduling agent comes to you and complains that he does not have enough people to place on the schedule. You tell him, "Hey, you guys wanted to be in charge of scheduling. Deal with it!" This happened at my place of employment. Supervision took advantage of the fact that they were relieved from scheduling responsibilities. They hid in the coffee shop and generally took longer breaks, while the employees often worked without a break at all. There were days when I got one three-minute break all day, which I really could not afford, but I had to go to the bathroom some time!

This example may seem like a contradiction. First we complained that supervision made all the decisions. But when they gave us responsibility to decide, we complained that they did not do anything to help us. What you should know is that there is a difference between being "bossy" and being a leader. If you delegate responsibility for a task that was previously yours, such as scheduling (even if the employees ask for it), it does not give you authority to hold out your hands and say, "Hey, you got what you wanted," when they complain. The leader must still be there for his team when they need him no matter what the situation. Passing the buck does not relieve you of responsibility. Passing the buck is like running over a bicyclist with your car and saying that it was not your fault that he died because he was not wearing a helmet! It is easy to pass the buck. Even worse is when it is done as openly and shamelessly as in the example described above.

JACK AND JILL WENT UP THE HILL

Now that you have had some time to let these ideas settle, the grand question is: Can human nature be changed, or is there even such a thing as human nature? Are we born to behave a certain way, or can our behavior be molded to fit a particular leadership model? The answer is that human nature cannot be changed because nature is by definition the inherent feature or characteristic of an organism, which in essence means that it cannot be changed. However, human behavior can be changed, but only at a considerable cost. If you do a risk/benefit analysis, you will most likely find that the price of change is often too great for the value. So if you cannot offer clever slogans and visits to the fish market to motivate people to change for the long haul, how do you know which leadership model to use and which leadership books have value? You start by doing a *Jack and Jill*.

Jack and Jill went up the hill . . . A very interesting law professor once taught me a most important leadership lesson that lies hidden in the first sentence of this simple nursery rhyme. Who are Jack and Jill? A boy and a girl, you say? How do you know? What if Jack is really Jacqueline? What if Jack is a jackass (a donkey)? How did Jack and Jill get up the hill? Did they walk, run, crawl, or bike? Did Jack carry Jill or did Jill carry Jack? How big is the hill? Is it a molehill or Mount Everest? Is the hill grassy, rocky, steep, or shallow? How long did it take Jack and Jill to get up the hill? Do the answers to these questions really matter?[128]

The value of an idea lies in the substance and not in the words. You must be specific and not general in your definition if you want your ideas to have meaning. To answer a question intelligently we need access to certain information about the central substance, or the gist of the thing discussed, which means that we must do a *Jack and Jill*, or ask pertinent questions for the purpose of defining the subject. In fact, on one of our exams in law class we were given a scenario and were graded on our ability to ask as many questions specifically pertaining to the scenario as possible, or to use a cliché: to leave no stone unturned. What I took from this is that our greatest pitfall is assumption: assuming that others think like you and like what you think; assuming that the right leadership or the right attitude can change people; assuming that we agree on what is right; assuming that bigger or more is better and smarter is better than harder; assuming that we agree on smarter; assuming that strength is in numbers; assuming that there is no "I" in team and together everybody achieves more; assuming that two heads think better than one, that there are no dumb questions, and that we should all move with the cheese; assuming that if it ain't broke there is still room for improvement; assuming that the customer is right; assuming that we all like to have fun and laughter is the best medicine; assuming that we agree on fun; assuming that proactive is better than reactive and today is the first day of the rest of your life; assuming that zero tolerance is productive or even possible; assuming that we all work toward the same goal; assuming that value-added, result-driven, quality-driven, and strategic fit have meaning; assuming that win-win is better than win-lose and half-full is better than half-empty; assuming that thinking outside the box is necessary and if nothing is ventured nothing is gained; assuming that the ballpark is safe; assuming that the ideas that empower you also empower others; assuming that people are responsive to empowerment or even know what it is; assuming that communication means exchanging verbal or written messages; assuming that it is everybody's responsibility; assuming that there really is a bottom line and that leaders are made, not born . . . Or is it the other way around?

It has been said that leadership mistakes made in the planning are the most difficult to forgive, because it often means that those affected are doomed before they even start. But since leadership theoreticians do not deal with the complex problems of life in the trenches, when reading leadership books whether for educational purposes or simply to pass time, how do you guard against stumbling into the wrong trench? You start by going a step beyond the obvious and taking possession of what you hear and see. The good leader comments and questions and speaks of what he or she knows from experience and gut feeling. The good leader seeks support from a team that is extraordinarily able and committed. The good leader does a *Jack and Jill* (a dissection of the meaning) on every problem and asks as many questions pertaining to the scenario as possible. The good leader acknowledges the fact that being politically correct often blurs one's vision. The good leader challenges himself or herself to see things as they are and do what is right.

Defining the steps along the way is important because definitions provide expectations of what the team will accomplish and open the door for questions and debate, which further aid the leader in fine-tuning the journey and help him avoid as many obstacles as possible. The leader who can restate a problem from the perspective of the opposition in a way that is satisfactory to *them* (not to the leader) can be reasonably assured that he has defined the problem and communicated it clearly. To take ownership of an idea, the leader must carry a thought to conclusion. Employees can likewise guard against manipulative practices conducted by the leadership by doing a *Jack and Jill*, or as has been said:

> He who does not know and does not know that he does not know is an idiot.

> He who does not know and knows that he does not know is uneducated.

> He who knows and does not know that he knows is sleepy.

> He who knows and knows that he knows is wise.

Let us move on and look at some situations you may experience as a team leader or team leader candidate. As we do so, think about how to ask the appropriate questions, how to leave no stone unturned; in short, how to do a *Jack and Jill* on every problem that comes your way.

A MATTER OF TIMING

Who becomes a leader? The leader is set apart from the rest; he is in his position because he has worked hard and is committed, and because he has certain qualities that will be helpful to the workers and the company. At least this is the way it is supposed to be. But in reality it is the people who choose their leader regardless of his or her official title. You do not become a leader by placing a "supervisor" patch on your shirt; you become a leader by exercising certain qualities that make others want to follow you. When I asked one of my supervisors if he could find me a roll of tape, he grouchily waved his hand and said that I could go and pick it up in the supply room. When I asked a different supervisor the same question, he looked up from his desk, smiled, and said, "I have now taken on the role of supply clerk." Three minutes later he came back with the tape. Which of these supervisors do you think received the higher score on my unofficial leadership evaluation? If you desire to Lead with War, remember that General Russel L. Honoré stated that logistics, or getting the supplies needed to do the job, are crucial for a team to succeed.

Now answer this question: How do you know that you are a team leader? Is it because it is in your job description? Is it because of that convincing little speech you held during your team leader interview? Is it because you have an outgoing personality and work well with others? Does your company require that you become a team leader before they allow you to climb to a higher position, because that is how the promotion chain works? Do you have to know how to lead people before you can manage things? Is leadership for everybody and can anybody learn it? Or can you be a great manager even if you are a poor team leader and vice versa? (Are leaders born or made?)

Imagine this: You are a manager interviewing a team leader candidate, and ask her to tell you about the most challenging situation she has ever experienced and how she resolved it. She answers, "I have never faced a situation that was a real challenge." Based on her answer, how do you know whether or not she is fit to be a leader? How do you determine, based on her answer, whether she is inexperienced, cocky, or deals so well with challenge that nothing is difficult? Perhaps she just lives a dull life? Although a good leader should not be abrasive, she does not need to be overly friendly either. Outgoing can translate into gung-ho and annoying. For example, you might translate a team leader's constant radio chatter as "excellent communication skills," and her bossiness as "great team player." But does the team feel the same? If she is too enthusiastic, her team might find her dominant or flaky or plainly irritating, and so, her enthusiasm will not rub off on the team. Will you hire her? How do you decide?

When hiring for a job opening, there is normally an elimination process that may involve education, background, experience, etc., with certain minimum requirements. But how do you know, once you have weeded out certain people, that the core group you are left with is really those who will do the best job for you? If you use pre-employment tests, they should be relevant to the job. For example, some companies require applicants for jobs that are physical in nature to pass an agility test. But does an agility test really measure what is important? I would personally much rather work with those who are less strong but have motivation and work ethics, than with those who are more strong but lack a desire to work. It is almost impossible to rate efficiency based on physical characteristics and educational background. People excel when they have a passion for the job.

When determining where somebody fits, you might want to start by looking at recurring patterns in his or her performance. Even qualities that initially seem undesirable, such as not working well with others, interrupting others in conversation, being impatient, or demanding that all work be finished an hour early, are not by nature bad qualities. They only become so when we misunderstand how to use them, or when we try to eradicate or change them instead of making good use of them.

Thus whether the wheel that squeaks gets the grease or whether silence is golden is a matter of timing. Whether a quiet person is a good or bad communicator is a matter of timing. A quiet leader is not necessarily afraid of telling his team what he wants them to do. Success is relative. You want a successful person to be part of your leadership team, but what determines success in your particular company? Is success measured by how much money the leader makes for himself or the company? Is success measured by how the leader's superiors or subordinates view him or her? Is success measured in matters unrelated to the job; for example, marriage and family, background and education, or health and fitness? Whose opinion is more important? Why? An academic degree is not an absolute necessity to achieve excellence in leadership, but it is necessary to know how people learn, how to solve problems and, in general, what makes your team tick. So what does make your team tick? If in doubt, the simplest way to find out is by asking them! This should be obvious but often is not. Should the leader be committed to the company or to the team or to both? The obvious answer is probably to both, but if you *had* to make a choice?

Now define the qualities of a good leader. But remember, as you brainstorm, that there is a danger: Listing everything that comes to mind does not mean that everything has merit. When we say that something is "everybody's responsibility," we diminish the value of the responsibility. When we say that a leader should be good at thirty different things, we likewise diminish the value of each of these things. As an example, let us say that you have a problem with safety, so you call on your employees and ask that each comes up with three things that would provide a safer work environment. If you have one-hundred people working for you, you would potentially get three-hundred answers. If you implemented them all, would you really achieve your objective of a safer work environment, or would you perhaps create a problem where there was none before? Focus should be placed on identifying "real" safety issues and correcting them in a timely manner. But to do that you must first identify the procedures that are actually causing a problem rather than helping it. Having too many procedures may in itself be a safety concern. Telling somebody what to do is easy; telling them how to do it is more difficult. Writing a long list of desired leadership qualities is easy; defining how it should be done is more difficult. To reach success with brainstorming, you need to discriminate.

So now, armed with a bit of background information about *Jack and Jill*, if you were to interview somebody for a team leader position, what questions would you ask? How do you picture the perfect team leader? What kinds of skills does he have? Be specific. Do not say good communication skills; rather say that he should hold a briefing once a day, listen to the concerns of the employees, and follow up the next day on questions or issues. The idea is not to come up with as many suggestions as possible, but to come up with the fewest number of good suggestions. When selecting a leader, this is your first opportunity to discriminate and narrow the list. For example, you might find the following attributes desirable leadership qualities:

1. A good leader is a team player.

2. A good leader identifies the objective and organizes a plan.

3. A good leader utilizes his team to reach the objective.

4. A good leader ensures that the team works with minimal friction toward the achievement of the goal.

Although this list is a good start, it fails to define the terms. What is team play? How does the leader go about identifying the objectives and organizing a plan? How does he motivate his team to reach the objectives, and how does he anticipate and minimize friction between team members? A team leader wants to be successful, but just exactly what is meant by the word success? Success to one person is not necessarily success to another. Each characteristic or issue should be defined and broken down into its component parts, until there is no question about its exact meaning. This exercise is a great confidence builder as well. Once you have defined every term for yourself, you can with confidence disagree with any issue that is discussed, because you will know exactly where you stand and why and thus be able to argue from a position of strength.

Furthermore, in job interviews or interviews for promotions the interviewer has sometimes decided beforehand, based on personal opinion, whether or not the applicant will be awarded the job. The applicant's performance in the interview therefore carries little weight. In cases where the interviewer does not know the applicant beforehand, the first impression may decide the outcome. The questions and answers used in the interview will then merely help rationalize why this person should or should not be hired. An applicant who takes the middle road, avoids the use of extremes, and maintains vagueness in his answers will give the interviewer an easy justification for hiring him. The opposite is also true: If the interviewer does not like a candidate based on his first impression, he can justify his decision not to hire the candidate through selective hearing; by hearing the answers he or she wishes to hear. These types of interviews are not objective. Before conducting a job interview with an applicant, find out how objective you are by asking yourself if the applicant's answers will really matter. If you knew nothing else about him or her, would you hire or not hire him based solely on his answers? If you cannot answer this question and keep your answer in mind throughout the interview, the interview will not be objective.

Objective questions must also be relevant. If the applicant gives you the answer you want, are you still certain that he would be a good candidate for the job? How do you know? Many answers fail to tell you much about a person's motivation or work ethics. Interviewers often ask about an applicant's background. But which is more important: asking what the applicant can do for the company, or simply verifying what he has already done? Why? Identifying what he has already done might demonstrate that he is trainable and hopefully has work ethics and vision. Selecting a good candidate for the job takes a willingness to challenge assumptions, even those coming from superiors, experts, or "reliable sources."

Thus rather than asking a candidate whether he or she is a team player, ask: "Tell me about a time when you applied the team player concept and the results." This will give you an idea of whether you and the candidate define "team play" the same. Many people also associate team play with outgoing personality and social skills. But what about the loner, the person who does not enjoy going to parties or only has few and select friends? The loner is often viewed as somebody who would not make a good leader.

Is this necessarily true? If you ask an applicant to tell you about a time when he or she had difficulty solving a problem, and he says that he has never had such an experience, does this mean that he is smug and cocky, that he is lying, or that he is telling the truth and is in fact a very efficient leader?

GONE FISHING (but not at the *Fish!* market in Seattle)

Now place yourself in the position of the team leader candidate. Once you are selected, you must know where you wish to take your team. If the interviewer asks what should be handled first: a message from an employee asking you to call him at home; a message from the manager asking you to report to him ASAP; or a situation where one of your employees has been injured on the job, what will you tell him? If you think about it, there really is not enough information to make a sound decision. The true answer to this question thus has to be a judgment call at the time it happens. To determine the urgency of the situation and make a sound decision, you must know, for example, if the employee injury in this hypothetical example happened right now or last week?

If the interviewer asks you how you resolved a really difficult situation, what will you tell him? Remember that the term "difficult" is subjective, and what is difficult for one person may be easy for another. What if he asks you to define the term team leader? Although it might appear as though a good team leader wears many hats (leader, friend, problem solver, and role model), he works primarily in a support role to the team. Rather than dictating how the work should be done, you might want to suggest that he should solicit information from the employees to fully utilize his resources.

Team play involves the ability to work well with others, which involves breaking barriers between different teams and departments. But why do these barriers form? If you said "yes" to team play, describe a time when you applied the team play concept and broke some barriers. But do not stop here. Think the thought to conclusion and also describe the results. If, on the other hand, you had let the barriers stand, what would you have achieved? Or would it even have mattered whether or not you broke barriers? Without further clarification, the list of desirable leadership qualities above is too weak to prove effective. Moreover, the image these leadership qualities paint in your mind most likely differs from the image they paint in somebody else's mind. For example, if a worker complains to you that the employees in a different department are lazy, and you say, "If you feel they've got it easier than you, then why don't you ask to work on their team next time?" how helpful do you think this reply is in breaking barriers? You have now become more about principle than about team play and will likely build barriers between yourself and your team rather than break them. A better way may be to ask why the laziness of the workers in the other department matters to your team. Once you understand where they are coming from, you can start forming a strategy for breaking the barrier.

Good leadership practices follow the model for learning: rote, understanding, application, correlation. **Rote** means that you can repeat back information by memory without understanding or being able to apply the information properly. **Understanding** means that you can explain the how and why of a situation but cannot necessarily perform proficiently. Although proficient performance comes with time and practice, proficient performance without understanding is mechanical and useless in a situation that requires adaptation. **Application** means that you can use the skill and perform tasks non-mechanically; it means that you can adapt by performing tasks under less than predictable circumstances. **Correlation** means that you can see how an issue *correlates* to another issue or to other material you have not yet learned. It means that you can use a skill intended for a specific task and apply it to another task without asking for help from others. All sources of information are valuable to the leader, but few are as valuable as those that help him or her use his knowledge to guide others.

> Application = Give a man a fish and he will eat for a day.
> Correlation = Teach a man to fish and he will eat for life.

Although specific techniques for performing a task can be taught, concepts are more difficult to teach. Intelligence is demonstrated through an understanding of the concepts and not through repetition of techniques, nor through the mindless repetition of popular slogans. Part of leadership thus encompasses mechanics of technique; the other part encompasses proper thinking. German philosopher Friedrich Nietzsche said, "What is great in man is that he is a bridge and not an end."[129] Next time you observe a member of your team using a different technique than the one called for when accomplishing a specific task, instead of correcting him, ask why. Then explain why or why not his technique has merit. Intelligence is also the ability to carry a thought to conclusion, or in simpler terms, to see the full picture; to see how one issue correlates to another.

And yes, there are dumb questions and also dumb answers. But above all there are dumb people. When I asked supervision why we were working so short handed, they said, "Because management is not filling the open lines." Well, yes, thank you, that is obvious. So why was management not filling the open lines? The answer: "Because we are short handed." Obviously the leader who gave me this reasoning did not know where he was going. Rather than walking in a circle, good leadership can be likened to a spiral staircase; you must be both in front of and behind your team at the same time. Lead from the front yet back them up not by walking in a circle, but by helping them climb closer to achieving the goal. This is also true regarding the reciprocal relationship between leader and team. If the leader stands behind the team's actions, the team will be more motivated to stand behind the leader's actions.

Now that we have an idea of the dangers of assumption and falling in lockstep with those who mouth popular slogans, let us examine in greater depth why using cheese, fish, and carrots as substitutes for real solutions to real problems can have disastrous consequences, and how to guard against the misuse, unintentional or otherwise, of popular slogans by management.

THOSE PESKY FOUR-LETTER WORDS

Motivational sayings are preached to us daily and posted on our walls, office doors, calendars, and day planners. But how many of these, "You manage things but lead people," have our leaders analyzed down to the component parts of the saying? How often have they actually done a *Jack and Jill* and asked the pertinent questions? How many of these sayings have really catapulted workers into great achievements rather than merely acted as a quick fix?

Years ago when my friend Bubba was going through a difficult divorce and suffered from stress and depression, his aunt said, "Chin up, Bubba, today is the first day of the rest of your life!" Initially this sounded like something I might have said to Bubba. But when he relayed the story to me I was ashamed, because Bubba taught me that the ridiculous saying has no basis in reality. Not only did it utterly fail to explain what exciting new possibilities lay beyond this "first day of the rest of your life," it failed to state how he was supposed to go about achieving them. More importantly, Bubba taught me that motivational sayings only work for those who are already motivated. Success through positive thinking has limits. Although a slogan may reinforce what you already believe, it will not help you make an about-face or feel better about an already bad situation. In other words, it is useless where real change or significant progress is needed. Consider the implications of the following statements:

1. There is always room for improvement.
2. Be proactive.
3. Be a team player.
4. Work smarter, not harder.

The idea that we can motivate people through euphemisms, or simply by assigning a positive meaning to a word, is disingenuous. Yet motivational books seldom question or explore to what extent we can fix a problem by changing somebody's attitude or assigning the problem a positive label. How often have you heard that there is always room for improvement; that setbacks are merely steppingstones to success; that failure is an opportunity for greatness; and the utterly untrue statement that what does not kill you makes you stronger? (Do you really think that a mother and father who lose their first child will really be psychologically stronger when expecting their second child? Do you really think that the thousands of soldiers who suffer from post traumatic stress disorder are really stronger thanks to their horrific experiences on the battlefield, simply because the war did not kill them?)

The statement, "There is always room for improvement," is a cliché that leads us to believe that simply rewording a problem gives us an opportunity to improve. But there is a difference between coming up with new ways of doing our job and coming up with new ways that actually improve things and make our job more efficient. Unless we have analyzed and measured in some tangible way exactly what needs to be done and how it will improve the current situation, saying that there is always room for improvement becomes rather meaningless. Change does not automatically bring improvement and doing more (or doing something) is not necessarily a measure of success.

Consider now the impact of "four-letter" words; you know, "don't" and "can't," which many motivational speakers, writers, and team leaders have said they would like to eliminate from our vocabulary. How many times have you been told that you should think positive and have a "can do" attitude? Yet the reason why the positive "do" has a greater impact than the negative "don't" is because of a principle of *learning*, and not because these words are inherently good and bad words that fuel or kill our motivation. It works like this: If you tell somebody to *do* something (such as, tell me your name, hand me that letter, etc.), his or her brain can immediately visualize what he is supposed to do. But if you tell him *not* to do something (such as, don't tell me your name, don't hand me that letter), his brain must first visualize what he is supposed to do (tell you his name, hand you the letter), before it can visualize what he is *not* supposed to do. This requires an extra step in the analytical process, which is why people seem to respond slower to the negative than the positive command. Let me demonstrate: Which of the following has greater impact?

1. Be proactive!
2. Don't be reactive!

Number one has greater impact but not because of the word "proactive," which is meaningless unless we assign it a meaning, but because of the sentence construction, which eliminates the extra step of having to visualize what one is supposed to be before one can visualize what one is not supposed to be. Now reverse it:

1. Be reactive!
2. Don't be proactive!

Which statement has greater impact? Which command is easier to visualize and follow? Still number one! Amazing, ain't it? Half-full is thus not inherently better than half-empty. Or as Sigmund Freud (1856-1939 CE) said, "Sometimes a cigar is just a cigar."[130] Real problems require real solutions, and whether the glass is half-full or half-empty is a matter of which direction the contents are flowing. If it is being filled, it is half-full; if it is being emptied, it is half-empty. If we do not know whether it is being filled or emptied, we do not have enough information to answer the question of whether it is half-full or half-empty. Simply assuming that a person who views the glass as half-empty has a negative attitude is insulting and demonstrates a lack of analytical capacity. Motivation comes through a desire to achieve something that has real value, and not through positive or negative commands.

Thus to determine whether something is good or bad, we must relate it to what we wish to achieve. Do is not inherently better than don't; can is not inherently better than can't; proactive is not inherently better than reactive; half-full is not inherently better than half-empty . . . Sunshine is not inherently better than rain. If we desire to get rid of what is in the glass, we would much rather view it as half-empty than half-full; if we have suffered a four-month drought, we would much rather have rain than sunshine. If we are going on a picnic, the reverse is true. Likewise, the four-letter words "don't" and "can't" do not automatically imply laziness, a bad attitude, or lack of confidence. After all, why should we all be overly zealous extroverts? Has it not also been said that silence is golden? Remember that your people could do a better job, *if* they wanted to. Your duty is not to make them do a better job, but to make them *want* to do a better job. *Want* is a four-letter word. When somebody says, "I can't do that," instead of saying, "Sure you can," or "You are so negative," ask, "What *can* you do?" or, "What do you *want* to do?"

Thus all four-letter words do not have the negative connotations of don't and can't. TEAM (Together Everybody Achieves More), for example, is a four-letter word and a popular one at that. Yet as previously mentioned, most people who mouth motivational slogans are simply repeating what they have read somewhere or heard at a motivational seminar they attended years ago. In short, they are using rote memorization without understanding. If I were to put you on the spot about the meaning of the TEAM acronym, my guess is that you would say something along the following lines: "You cannot place yourself ahead of the team, the team is more important than the individual, all for one and one for all, therefore, together everybody achieves more." But how do you know that what you just said is true and has merit? Besides, "all for one" sounds like communism to me.

To be effective, a leader must draw a following; he must know what is to be achieved and how to get there. The TEAM acronym fails on both counts. Together . . . how? Everybody . . . who? Achieves more . . . of what? As an employee, next time you go to work, pay attention to when sayings like these tend to appear, and you will likely find that it is not after great success has been reached that the leadership posts motivational bullshit on the walls, but rather when there are personnel issues they would rather not confront directly, such as impending cutbacks in salaries and personnel. When you already feel good about yesterday's accomplishments, the TEAM acronym may reinforce what you already know. But after weeks, months, or even years of obstacles seemingly without end, how effective is the same saying that motivated you yesteryear?

Furthermore, to speak the truth, we need to see things as they are rather than as we wish them to be. Assigning a higher meaning to a word does not make it so. Using "displaced" rather than "bumped" does not make it hurt less when you lose your job. Or as martial arts expert Ed Parker (1940-1973 CE) reminded us: "[T]he spelling or pronunciation of the word designating self-defense does not add nor subtract from its effectiveness. In the case of the word 'punch,' in foreign language classes, it is spelled and pronounced differently. Yet, no matter what spelling or pronunciation it is given, it still hurts when it is delivered."[131] After taking a deep pay cut, how often have you heard people say, "Well, at least I've got a job"? Yes, it is better to be healthy and rich than sick and poor, as my grandfather used to say. But if you are sick and poor, it is better to acknowledge that you are sick and poor than pretend otherwise and fail to strive for a better future.

THE EMPTY SUIT

Although a job that presents opportunities for initiative and growth can enrich your life, as we have seen, a person who is not motivated by competition, or personal praise, or teamwork, or free tickets to a football game, will not respond to your grand plans. Everybody does not respond to the same type of motivation. If you want to use motivation to catapult your employees upward, you must also understand their passions, loves, goals, and desires. Furthermore, to inspire others, you must be watchful of certain motivation killers. For example, if you assign the most efficient employees the most difficult tasks or give them the heaviest workload simply because you know that the work will get done, you are in effect rewarding the slackers and punishing the good workers. Likewise, a certain motivation killer is asking an employee who finishes a task early to help other employees who constantly finish late, some of whom were most certainly wasting time.[132]

Now answer this question: There is a less than desirable job to be done, and you have two people who can do it. One is a star employee with a great deal of intelligence and great work ethics. You know that if you place him on the job, the job will get done. The other is a less talented employee, who often shows up late and does less than his share. In fact, he does barely enough to get by. What should you do? At one place of employment, this was a consistent problem. The best employees were doing the worst jobs, and over a period of months or years it wore them out. They were not happy anymore. Remember that an employee must feel good about working to be motivated. Yet when they asked the team leader why they were always placed in the worst positions, the answer was, "Because you are so good at it." Is this really the best strategy?

The reasoning may initially seem sound, because if you put the best people on the worst job, your stats will be met and your superiors will be happy. While if you put the worst people on the worst job, the reverse is true and you will have some explaining to do to higher ups. But what does this do to the attitudes of your best people? Perhaps a talented employee could excel even more if he were placed in a position that truly interested him? What about the less talented employee? Just how should the workload be divided? Should the most talented employee get the best job as a reward for being who he is? Should the less talented employee be punished with the worst job? If somebody performs poorly, should you train him so that he can perform better, or should you place him in another position that might interest him more? Do you build on people's strengths, or do you try to eliminate their weaknesses? These are not easy questions to answer, but they matter and should be asked if you desire to gain insight into leadership. Finding a person's talents also requires that you are truly interested in finding his or her talents. In other words, you must care about him more than you care about your title.

An employee might prefer to work alone in a position where he can be the sole person responsible for organizing and planning the work. If this is his strength, would arguing that he is not a team player make him more efficient? If you really want to see a person shine, you must place him in a position where he can use his talents. No talent becomes evident until preparation and opportunity meet. Having the opportunity to use the talent is at least as important as having the talent itself. If the opportunity is not there, you will never know how talented the person is. How do you know what a person's talents are? Well, you can observe and make that determination over time. However, it might be easier to ask him or her directly. For example, you might see somebody type away at the computer at a hundred words a minute, and therefore feel that this person should be placed in a position that requires a lot of typing. But if he or she does not have the desire to work in the position you have in mind, you will do more harm than good by placing him there. The employee is the ultimate judge of what position is right for him or her. The best you can do is to question and guide.

The main obstacle to motivation is lack of desire. Others include:

1. Unfair treatment or critique. Fairness does not necessarily mean that everybody is treated exactly the same, and critique is not in itself an obstacle to motivation. In fact, it could be

a catalyst, but the person critiqued must understand and agree with the critique.

2. Leader lack of interest, or appearing uninterested even if he or she is interested. If you have other things on your mind, you must still appear interested in front of your team or explain the reasons for your apparent lack of interest.

3. Physical discomfort or illness. A person who is sick or carries mental baggage must satisfy his personal needs first. A friend once told me, "If it ain't right at home, it ain't right at work either."

4. Apathy caused by inadequate preparation or inability to organize. Leader inability to take the efforts of the team seriously is a contributor to apathy.

5. Change. When change occurs, more than one person is affected. All those affected by the change must therefore know that their feelings are respected. Including your team in discussions for change can help alleviate this obstacle.

Motivational factors must also be challenging, achievable, and desirable. The manager who hung miniature hardhats in the door openings where Bubba worked was destined for failure, because not only did she fail to define the goals (she expected the employees to set their own goals without even asking if they were interested in setting goals), by failing to define, no one knew if the goals were desirable or even achievable. If the goals of the company and the goals of the individuals do not coincide, the goals cannot be used as motivators. Motivation also needs timing. The team must be ready to peak in order to peak. If the team lacks the necessary physical resources or carries significant mental baggage, you must choose a better time for presenting the motivating factor.

During a recent economic crisis, customer service at one company dwindled to the point that something had to be done to "teach" the workers the value of customer service. The company sent each employee to a one-day seminar that was a complete failure, because the employees' minds were not on customer service but on how to care for their families during pay cuts and layoffs. In fact, the employees were so angry that the seminar facilitator, a twenty-year employee of the company, was brought to tears. This is called poor timing, and the results should have been anticipated. Just as we must satisfy our basic needs for food and shelter before we can satisfy our need for self-actualization, we must provide a solid base in the work environment before we can expect better performance. Before you can ask people to give, you must provide them with what they need: equipment, praise, opportunity, someone who cares. Once a person has these commodities, he will be more receptive to working hard and providing great customer service.

So let us say that you have managed to motivate the team to work efficiently, how do you preserve the hunger? Once motivation is achieved, it needs reinforcement and approval. A skillful leader can build enthusiasm by helping the individual perform successfully in front of his or her peers. Motivation also needs a concrete goal. Saying that "every day is a great day," or that you should "do something today that makes a customer smile," are weak motivators. Tangible goals, by contrast, heighten awareness and curiosity. Your team must also want to win. This may seem obvious, but if the team members cannot care less whether they win or lose, not much will get done.

Rather than assuming that we all want to win, the question you should ask is this: What motivates the team to want to win? If winning does not come with a reward of some sort, if it carries no greater weight than losing, then why should the employees put forth the extra effort it takes to win? How do you define winning, anyway? Does everybody on the team agree with the definition? Tangible returns that are meaningful such as a bonus or an extra day off with pay, carry greater weight than intangible returns such as a "thank you" (although a "thank you" is nice, too, and is part of common courtesy). The moment you sense that you are losing the team, stop and remember that this is their career, too. Finally, as already emphasized, motivation needs ownership. This is why it matters who gets the credit. How do we know?

Let us revisit the famous quote by American president

Harry S. Truman: "It is amazing what you can accomplish, if you do not care who gets the credit." This sounds like a great quote. However, if your achievements are not acknowledged and you know in advance that they will not be acknowledged, how motivated will you be to put forth the effort? If you write a great book and somebody else is listed as the author, how much motivation will you have to write another great book? If you have studied the martial arts for twenty years but do not get to wear a black belt, even though others who have only studied for a year or two wear black belts, how motivated will you be to pursue your studies? Perhaps equally important, how helpful can you be to others when they do not know who you are or what you have accomplished? Getting credit for your achievements is absolutely necessary, because others are more likely to come to you for answers or advice when they know your background, knowledge, and achievements. When you graduate from college, do you not want a certificate to hang on your wall? Do you not want to be able to state your achievements on a job application to secure a better job or higher salary?

To get the most out of Harry S. Truman's statement (or any statement or slogan for that matter), we must examine it within the context of our own times and circumstances. Remember that history does NOT repeat itself. Just because a particular statement was true for a particular person at a particular time, it is not true for all people at all times. "Need modifies law," said Swedish king Gustav Vasa (1496-1560 CE), "not only men's law, but occasionally God's law."[133]

Motivation must include more than empty words. By all means, set lofty goals, but do not present the team with an "empty suit." Speak the truth and identify the steps. Goals must be valuable to the individuals who make up the team, and my goals are not always your goals. How do you know that your goals or the proposed achievement has meaning to your team? You ask them. If your company's goal is "to become the world wide company of choice," and you are merely a lowly grunt, what specific images come to mind when you hear this goal stated, and why should you care? Why or why not does the goal motivate you? Exactly how does achieving the goal benefit you in particular? Most importantly, as the Greek critic and philosopher Aristotle (384-322 BCE) reminded us, goals must have duration and you must feel their impact every day: "For one swallow does not make a summer, nor does one fine day; and so too one day, or a short time, does not make a man blessed and happy."[134]

COSMIC CLAUSE VISION

Once the goals have been set, the vision must remain in view, because few people will find meaning in the journey alone without the promise or hope for something "better." If you feel as though you have been in the same ol' grind for twenty years, you probably have. A cosmic clause vision—a vision that is absolute or all encompassing in time and space, such as the "world's greatest"—is difficult to define and identify with and can therefore not serve as a great motivational factor. Being the greatest for the sake of being the greatest is meaningless. A better way is to state which specific part of the competition you need to beat and why. Doing so creates purpose and gives your team a goal to work toward which, in turn, makes it easier to choose an appropriate course of action.

Furthermore, similarly to the problem with saying that "it is everybody's responsibility," because this makes it, in effect, nobody's responsibility because nobody will feel ownership, a vision statement must appeal to somebody in particular and not to everybody. Imagine trying to advertise this book as:

1. Equally good for leaders and followers of any company throughout the world.

2. Infinitely valuable to professional leaders, those coming up through the ranks, teams and employees, and everyday people alike.

3. Everything you ever needed to know and ever will need to know about any leadership situation at any time.

Which of the above statements did you choose? Which one gave you the greatest insight into what this book is really about? Which one made the book marketable? The answer is, probably none. Why? Because none of the statements appeals to anyone in particular. If you say that housekeeping is everybody's responsibility, do you really think that the break room at your company will be spotless at the end of the shift each day?

So what exactly is your vision? Whoever is first in line must know where we are going, right? And to end up where you want to go, you must know where you are right now. Moreover, not liking what you have but not knowing what you want makes navigation difficult. Many leaders have a theoretical understanding of what they want to achieve. The problems start when they have to translate theories into actions. Suppose that your company recently stated its vision in writing—To Become the World's Greatest—and printed pocket-size handouts for the employees as reminders. Is becoming the world's greatest a good vision? Obviously you cannot do much better than the world's greatest, so the vision certainly gives you something to strive toward. But on your road to becoming the greatest, where do you start?

Your vision will not be achievable unless you can state the goal in concrete terms and why it is important that you achieve it. Your vision statement should tell you who you are and where you want to go. The vision, "to become the world's greatest," is weak because it fails to define who you are, who you need to defeat, and what you must do to reach your objective. In practical terms, it is as useful (or useless) as "to become a millionaire" or "to understand the meaning of life." If you do a *Jack and Jill* on the vision, you will no doubt achieve greater clarity. How do you define "greatest"? According to what criteria, and who is the judge? The world's greatest . . . In size? In service? In revenue? Next, who determines the size and scope of the "world"? Do you really need to serve every country on the globe to be the world's greatest, or is there some leeway here? What is the purpose of becoming the world's greatest, anyway? Why is it a worthwhile vision? Simply hanging inspirational posters on the wall and including a line or two in your vision statement about integrity and dazzling customer service do not make it so.

So let us try again, how good do we want to be? We want to be *very* good. Okay, so what? What does *very* mean? How about *very, very* good! Do you feel any smarter? I don't. Upon reaching the vision, we want our customers to be *very* happy. We also want our employees to be *very* happy. Very has a different meaning to different people. How rich do you want to be? I want to be *very* rich. Yeah, but . . . ? If your vision is to "nurture and encourage the (your company's name) culture," or to "find creative, new, and efficient ways of doing business," explain what the culture is and how to be creative. If your vision is to "be the biggest in the industry," or to "be the customer's number one choice," define biggest and explain what the customers want, and how you know that this is what they want. A problem with many motivational sayings is that nobody explains how to use them.

To prove meaningful, the vision must also be agreed upon and achievable within a reasonable timeframe. Think about this: Becoming the "world's greatest," is a vision that is not only difficult to define, it may not be attainable at all, at least not within the scope of the specific careers of your employees, so why should they care? How do you know that the vision is achievable? You know when you break it down into tangible steps. (Tangible = that which can be touched, felt, understood, and identified with.) It is better to present two or three definite steps than a list of twenty concepts. Rather than striving to become the greatest, you might want to state a slightly less valuable, yet more precise and achievable goal, knowing that it is a steppingstone toward the loftier vision.

Strategy is your plan and tactics are the particular steps you take or the means you use to realize your strategy. If you have a strategy but no tactics, your vision will remain on the drawing table; it will never be realized. If you have tactics but no strategy; your vision will become a trial and error type endeavor. Adhering to your strategy may mean the difference between success and failure. Or as they say in aviation: Plan your flight and fly your plan. Your strategy keeps you on track and helps you avoid stepping off the charted course. Your tactics take you step-by-step closer to reaching your goal.

Thus without a clearly defined goal and clearly defined steps, your vision, and thus your job, is nothing but a necessary evil that you partake in solely for the purpose of paying your bills. Few people will find meaning in the journey alone, with no promise or hope of a reward at the end of the tunnel. The same goes for your vision. If you cannot list the steps required to get there (wherever "there" is), the vision will have little value. If the vision is not desirable, it will have little value. You must also have ownership of the vision; you must have reasonable control of the journey. The team must thus be updated on its progress. When evaluating how far you have come, be precise and avoid abstract words such as "we can" or "we know." Do not say, "We are way ahead of where we were this time last month." Give the team concrete evidence instead.

When you have defined the vision in concrete terms, continue by identifying the obstacles. Is this not negative thinking? Should we not state what we should and can do rather than talk about what stands in our way? "A chief of state does not want to hear a general in the field say that he 'hopes' to win tomorrow's battle or that he's 'visualizing victory'; he or she wants one whose plans include the possibility that things may go very badly, and fall-back positions in case they do. Even that ultra-optimistic president Ronald Reagan invoked realism when dealing with the Soviets, constantly repeating the slogan 'Trust, but verify.'"[135] Remember that much of your motivation stems from the competition: Another's greatness can serve as a catalyst for your own.

Now consider what is wrong with these objectives and what barriers might stand in your way:

1. To make my team the best that it can be

2. To turn my company into a world-class champion

3. To make every customer smile

4. To build a company operated by people whose commitment ensures that customers will return for all of their future business needs

Now do a *Jack and Jill*: What does it take to be the best? If you are the best that you can be, will it be enough to outdo the competition? Remember that you *must* win. How do you know where your limits are, anyway? What is meant by world-class? Is every customer really *every* customer, or just the majority? Why is it important that they smile? How do you achieve this? Without identifying the steps and the obstacles, the objective is meaningless. And being the best that you can be is meaningless if the competition is better.

One company recently issued a memo stating, "Each workgroup reviewed ranks near the top of the industry, and is projected to rank number two or three by the end of the year." Oh, did I tell you I just took second place? Good or bad? Taking second place is, in itself, neither good nor bad. We cannot make that determination unless we also know how many people were in the race. If it were just two, taking second place is not particularly admirable. If it were a thousand, taking second place is pretty darn good. Now do a *Jack and Jill*: What does it mean that each workgroup ranks number two or three if we do not also know how many contestants are in the race? When we cannot measure ourselves against tangible evidence, visualizing the next step becomes difficult.

The following sayings recently appeared on the walls at one workplace:

1. What have you done today that exceeded customer expectations?

2. Be proud. We are the world's greatest.

Let us look at number one first: Who is the judge? If you do not ask the customer what their expectations are, you have no way of knowing whether or not you have exceeded customer expectations. Now look at number two: Telling you that we are the world's greatest introduces an element of doubt; it implies that we are in fact *not* the world's greatest. If we were, we would have no need to say it. The natural development is to ask: Are we really the greatest? How do we know? And if not, then who is, and why? What constitutes great? Precision in definition is important if you want to present your employees with a roadmap that is void of confusion. You would be more successful if you said, "Our stock went up, the customers praised us publicly on national television, and you have a pay raise coming. Be proud. We are the world's greatest!"

Let us say that you reach your vision. Now what? What should you do once you get there? Is it enough to just barely become the greatest, or do you need to stay there and maintain a stronghold against the competition for time and eternity? And, if so, how? When setting goals or stating your vision, try to see what is beyond it. Your vision should not be the end result; it should be a steppingstone toward higher ground. If you ask "why" and "what next" before you get there, much of your journey will already be staked out. Doing so will also help clarify if achieving the goal is going to cost you more than you are willing to pay, and if the achievement will be as valuable as you thought. It might make you more open toward considering other more profitable alternatives. Might there be times when it is prudent to cut your losses and run, to abandon the vision or objective for the sake of saving the company or the team? Or is it true that reaching the objective is not about feeling good but about getting it done? If you answered "yes," give an example. If you answered "no," know why. When taking the first step, as Prussian military strategist Carl von Clausewitz said, also think about what might be the last.[136]

Part III

Leading with Science

"The important thing in science is not so much to obtain new facts as to discover new ways of thinking about them."

— Sir William Bragg

"Every great scientific truth goes through three stages. First, people say it conflicts with the Bible; next, they say it has been discovered before; lastly, they say they always believed it."

— Louis Agassiz

"For we study strategy as a science: the application of that knowledge is an art."

— Colonel Ned B. Rehkopf

A LESSON IN LOGIC AND TRUTH

Science is fascinating not because of the discoveries but because of the predictability; finding that the truth is in fact logic and steadfast, and that the concepts that were true a thousand years ago and earlier are still true today and most likely will be true tomorrow.[137] The leader who knows the truth and sees the evidence will have no problem foregoing debate and accepting the conclusion. He or she can enjoy the benefit of doing things right from the beginning. By contrast, the leader who fails to use science and logic to convince his or her team of a particular problem will come across as unintelligent or irrational. He or she will risk creating a chain reaction of strategic mistakes that may take years to fix, or that cannot be fixed.

Science involves the discovery of evidence and relationships; it demonstrates why things work the way they do. Technology gives us the tools and procedures. Science gives us a clear field of vision. Technology allows us to pursue our goals without second-guessing the outcome of our actions. Scientific principles used as analogies for leadership can teach a number of important concepts. For example, in the physical sciences a wave is defined as the transfer of energy from the source to a distant receiver. Wave motion can reveal something about the source: If a stone is dropped into a pond of water, waves will travel outward in expanding circles. But if two stones are dropped into the water, the waves produced by each stone can overlap and form an interference pattern. Within this pattern, wave effects may increase, decrease, or be neutralized. In other words, the two wave patterns can create a mutual reinforcement in some areas and a cancellation in others. When the crest of one wave overlaps the crest of another, the individual effects are added and called *constructive interference*. A leadership analogy can now be created: The two waves have "team worked" and produced an overall stronger wave.

The term *constructive* can be misleading, however. In the conceptual sense, an overall stronger "wave" does not necessarily translate into an overall more positive or efficient workforce. Depending on the circumstances and on what one is trying to achieve, *destructive interference* where the disturbance is minimized and the wave pattern flattened may, in fact, have a more constructive effect in the work environment. The careful observer, whether supervisor or employee, will do himself and the team a service by carefully analyzing how he applies scientific analogies to team leadership.

According to Webster's New World College Dictionary, a definition of *science* is "systematized knowledge derived from observation, study, and experimentation carried on in order to determine the nature or principles of what is being studied." This might be a good time to remember *Jack and Jill*. To truly form a rational opinion of the usefulness of science as a leadership tool, ask: What kind of knowledge? Systematized in what way and for what purpose? How were the observations, studies, and experiments conducted? What is meant by nature or principles? What is leadership, anyway? *What if* the leader relies on science to encourage cooperation and construct a desirable outcome, but really does not know where he is going?

The danger with Leading with Science is that the use of scientific principles presupposes a leadership style that is based on specific techniques and thus remains unaltered by innovation. The fundamental principle of logic states that if the premises (the examples that set it up) are true, the conclusion will automatically follow. Let me illustrate through the following example:

Premise 1:   if $A = B$
Premise 2:   and $B = C$
Conclusion: then $A = C$

Since A and B are equal, and B and C are equal, you simply exchange B for C to derive your answer. Anybody reasonable acquainted with Math 101 will see that this is true. Even an educated guess will assist the leader more often than not in making sound decisions. However, if the given information (the premises) is incorrect or misleading, setting up an equation for leadership and following it blindly because "science says it is supposed to work" predestines one for failure. Before accepting the science the leader must make an effort to determine the validity of the premises and weed out any information that is insufficient or irrelevant. When setting up examples in logic argumentation for the purpose of leadership, *even if* the premises are true the conclusion may NOT automatically follow. When dealing with people sometimes common sense trumps scientific evidence:

True

if A = B
and B = C
then A = C

False

if **A**dam loves **B**ridgette
and **B**ridgette loves **C**hristopher
then **A**dam loves **C**hristopher

Although it could be true that Adam loves Christopher, it is most likely false. When human emotions are involved, all logic is not true and all truth is not logic. How the leader feels about you, and how you feel about a particular issue, often determines whether or not you will cooperate and follow the leader regardless of whether or not the problem can be stated from a position of science. Thus passion often overrules logic and action must be guided by appropriate recognition of feelings. For example, if the leader treats an employee poorly perhaps by making a derogatory remark behind the employee's back, and later apologizes, unless he is also sincere in his apology, the damage cannot be repaired even if we agree in principle that an apology neutralizes an insult.

With few exceptions most conflicts are issues of passion. Even wars and world events are often issues of passion and not necessity. A team leader can therefore be passionate about an issue such as the necessity to wear a safety vest at work. But the employees can be equally passionate about not wanting to wear a safety vest. If no injuries have happened to those who do not wear the vest, and no injuries have happened to those who wear the vest, then who is correct? Does the safety vest really help prevent injuries, or do we merely think that it makes sense that it should so therefore it is mandatory to wear it? I am not arguing against safety vests or any other safety related issue, but merely demonstrating a point with respect to logic and truth. These sorts of issues can easily become a matter of who is right rather than what is right. Understanding the emotional part of human nature no matter how illogical may be the most important part related to success in leadership. As previously stated, it is important to remember that people are people first before they are workers, employees, or team members. People have emotions and when their emotions are upset they are not likely to respond to anything the leader has to say. Thus before you can repair a problem you must repair the damaged emotions.

How do you guard against following logic blindly without considering whether or not it is really "truth"? You take an educated guess. If Adam loves Bridgette, and Bridgette loves Christopher, does it really make sense to say that Adam loves Christopher? When I learned how to solve equations and other mathematical problems in school, I also learned another important lesson that has saved me many times from taking the wrong fork in the road. My teacher said, "Before you do the math (the science), step back and ask what would make sense. When you have done the calculations and before insisting on the conclusion, step back and ask if it makes sense."

As a pilot and flight instructor I have applied this advice in aviation when calculating course and heading. Pilots of small aircraft use a type of plastic ruler called a plotter for this purpose, taking magnetic variation and, later, wind speed and direction into account to establish the heading. However, if you are not observant you might read the reciprocal of your course on the plotter. To avoid this mistake I made a habit of taking an educated guess before making the actual calculations. For example, if I were going in the general direction of west, I might have guessed that the course would be somewhere in the neighborhood of 285 degrees. When I did the calculations, if it turned out to be 72 degrees, I would know that I had made a mistake and used the reciprocal because the answer was too far removed from my educated guess.

If, on the other hand, my calculations gave me a number of 252 degrees, I would know that it was probably correct because, even though it differed from my educated guess by some 30 degrees, it was still in the same general direction. If you are faced with a math problem, say 7 X 8, and you plug it into the calculator and get an answer of 5.6, it should send a warning signal. If you had taken an educated guess first, you would have known that the answer calls for a much larger number.

Here is another example of why one must understand the difference between logic and truth: The FAA (Federal Aviation Administration) requires that flight instructors renew their instructor license every other year. The requirement for renewal is either taking a refresher course and a written exam, or recommending at least ten students for their pilot's license exam with 80 percent passing the test. In my first two years as a flight instructor, I recommended eight students for their pilot's license tests and all of them passed; in other words, 100 percent passed. When time came to renew my instructor license, I went to the FAA office and asked the following question: "The requirement is ten students with 80 percent passing. I have signed off eight students with 100 percent passing. If you sign off ten students and eight of them pass, it is essentially the same as if you sign off eight students and eight pass. The end result in both cases is eight students passing the exam. Can I get my license renewed without taking the flight instructor refresher course?"

The FAA official scratched his head and said that he had never heard this argument before. Then he searched in the big book of regulations for an answer. When he found none, he said, "I am going to let common sense prevail and renew your license." The truth was that I had not signed off the required ten students; the logic was that I had achieved the requirement of eight students passing the test. Truth and logic were in conflict. When truth and logic conflict, rely on common sense. Even when a good plan has been carefully crafted and defined and leads to its logical conclusion, a leader who fails to cater to human emotions will likely alienate the team. As has been demonstrated, logic and truth are not the same. All logic is not true, and all truth is not logic.

What should be learned is that human relationships such as those that exist at the workplace deal heavily in emotions such as love, joy, fear, anger, and frustration. These emotions determine attitudes. You can therefore not approach human emotions like you do a mathematical equation. Still, we often attempt to do just this. We claim that if people only worked together a little better, we would have a more productive environment. But if the particular people in question do not like each other, for whatever reason, they will not work well together no matter how much you wish it were so, and no matter how much "science" and statistics demonstrate that people who work well together are more productive.

As another example, and as demonstrated in the previous section of this book, we can try to convince the workforce that they should enjoy change, because change takes us away from the same mundane grind every day. However, although this might be a logical thing to say, as we have seen, it is not logical in the sense of human emotion. Most people resist change unless the change actually originated with them. This does not mean that the rules of logic are completely wasted when dealing with people, but it does mean that for the rules to prove useful you must understand the concepts behind logic argumentation, which state that to get people to agree with the conclusion, they we must first agree with the premises. But even then, as seen in the "If A = B" example, there will be times when logic will fall flat on its face.

What factors should you be watchful of when applying scientific or rational thinking to your leadership style? A good place to start when considering how to answer this question is by doing a *Jack and Jill*, because this decreases the risk that you will act on impulse when trying to implement a new procedure. *Jack and Jill* will also help you detect incorrect information that masquerades as fact and may lead you down a faulty path. Finding one possible solution to your problem does not automatically exclude other possibilities. And do not forget to factor in uncertainty. Finally, remember that temporarily winning a heart through a clever slogan or a gung-ho speech is easy, but a broken spirit is difficult to heal.

Asking the pertinent questions is thus a prerequisite for gaining insight into the science of leadership. Those who fail to ask questions cannot lead others, because even if they know where they want to go they will not know how to get there, what happens if they take the wrong fork in the road, or how to correct a problem. Followers often ask more questions than leaders. Why? Because many leaders feel their job is to command rather than lead. Unfortunately for the leaders, this makes for a tough uphill battle. "I have taken all knowledge to be my province," said English statesman and philosopher Sir Francis Bacon (1561-1626 CE).[138] Never say "no thanks" to information. Accept what is handed to you, and decide later which parts you will take to heart and which parts you will discard. Let us move forward and talk about why the scientific method is such a valuable asset to science, and to what extent we can use it in the science and art of leadership.

THE SCIENTIFIC METHOD

A fact is a close agreement between competent people with respect to a series of observations of the same phenomenon. The catch is that the observers cannot be anybody; they must be competent. After you have defined competence, your first question might be how competence is established. Next you need a series of observations. Observing something once does not help you establish a fact. You must also consider the frame of reference, which is defined as a vantage point with respect to the position and motion of an object. Depending on where you stand, your frame of reference may differ from somebody else's. You may not see what somebody else sees and may therefore make false assumptions. In a scientific sense this idea can be related to *parallax*, which we will talk more about a little later.

To even begin to solve a problem, you must be curious enough to want to experiment with it. The issue must be on your mind enough that you feel a legitimate need to do something about it. How do you determine if your need is legitimate? It is easy to fall prey to our own capacity to fool ourselves. Some leaders are so certain that an issue needs to be addressed or changed that they decide on a solution before running it through the required steps of scientific analysis. Physical scientists, by contrast, approach problems from an unbiased standpoint; they abstain from deciding beforehand what science is to reveal. In fact:

> [T]he true mark of science (as opposed to its many masquerades) is an attempt to refute one's hypothesis, to be self-critical, to examine one's assumptions, and to point out ways to further test one's theory . . . Science makes probabilistic claims; it is not usually about proving that something is always the case, or never the case. Almost all science is about showing a greater probability that something is usually the case . . . The preponderance of the evidence represents scientific knowledge.[139]

To fully appreciate the laws of science and leadership, you must understand the rules. If you skip a step or work in reverse, you will create a chain reaction of strategic mistakes that may take years to fix, or that cannot be fixed. If you implement plans and procedures without truly understanding the underlying reasons, you will lose the trust of your team, be predestined for failure, and later try to save face when your team has thrashed you. The scientific method is a good place to start because it sort of covers your bases. How does it work? First recognize that you have a problem. If you do not know that you have a problem, it will be difficult to solve it. Next make an educated guess. The guess must be reasonably related to the problem. Then predict the consequences. This is called forming a *hypothesis*. When you have made an educated guess, forming the hypothesis is easier. Then test the hypothesis to determine if your educated guess has merit and your prediction is valid. Finally formulate a rule as simple and straight forward as possible intended to correct the problem.

Although scientific principles are great teachers, when searching for the science (the discovery of evidence and relationships) all hypotheses (the predictions of the consequences) must be testable. In other words, for the predictions to be valid there must be a way of proving them wrong. For example, if you work in the service industry, you might be inclined to implement a rule that requires your employees to address the customers by name. Your prediction is that doing so will foster a friendly atmosphere that benefits your business interests. Your next step is to perform an experiment to test the hypothesis. You give each customer a questionnaire asking whether they are more or less likely to do business with you as a result of being addressed by name. You now have your employees test the rule, record the findings over a period of time, and compare the results to those you acquired prior to the new rule taking effect.

You may now have constructed a test that will help you determine if the implementation of the new rule will help or hinder your business. The test is valid because the questionnaire and the employee testing of the rule over time have provided a way of proving your predictions wrong. Your predictions do not *have* to be proven wrong, but *there must be a way* of proving them wrong for the test to be valid in a scientific sense. For example, if you saw no change or if you saw a decline in business when the rule of addressing the customer by name was brought into effect, you would scrap the rule. By contrast, if the questionnaire did not provide the customer with a way of voicing a negative opinion, and if you neglected to run a comparison of results, you would not have provided the test subjects with a way of proving the hypothesis wrong. You would therefore not have gained any insight into the validity of the new procedure, at least not in a scientific sense.

Consider this: A common irritant when phoning a company for help is that you have to listen to a recording which states that "for quality assurance, this call may be monitored." Then you have to press one for English or two for Spanish. Then you will get a lengthy menu from which to choose a suitable action. Since many callers will be more than a little annoyed by now, the company's goal of customer satisfaction through monitoring the phone calls is defeated by the recording that says so and by the lengthy recorded menus. If you are an employee forced to address the customer by name or say, "Thanks for choosing (enter your company name here)," and are rated on how well you use this script, if the script fails to make the customer feel greater satisfaction it defeats the purpose. In fact, reading a script could have the effect of making the customer believe that you are incapable of or uninterested in showing genuine concern for his or her problems. You can also misuse the scientific method by leaving out steps, reversing the chain, or failing to ask the proper questions. For example, if you *assume* that people will turn to your business when they are addressed by name (perhaps because you like to be addressed by name), but you never actually run the experiments or ask why, you may or may not be correct in your assumption, but either way, you have not gained any true insight that you can use to your benefit later.

The ability to properly discern scientific relationships is often the result of an enormous amount of knowledge. Intellectual growth comes from the encouragement of open-minded debate, not from the memorization of and ability to restate the principles. For example, if you desire to change employee attitudes toward their jobs, it is insufficient to acknowledge that the goals of the company must coincide with the goals of the employees. You must go a step further and finish the thought by defining exactly what those goals are. You might also want to run your vision through some logic argumentation to determine if the employees and the company in fact agree on the premises. As demonstrated in the equation involving Adam, Bridgette, and Christopher, a system that is so rigid that it makes no allowances for human emotions tends to make leadership science meaningless.

Although the scientific method is a good place to start, it is not the only place. You can also make an effort to understand what those opposed to an idea are really saying. When analyzing a problem, learn to distinguish between what you see and what you wish to see. Be ready to accept your findings even if they are not what you wish them to be. When you refrain from shielding yourself from those opposing your ideas and instead strive to understand them in the proper context, you will set yourself up for intellectual growth. You do not have to do everything that your opposition is asking of you, but you do have to understand it. A principle may be a starting point as long as it is open to critique. When employees are allowed to critique widely, we eliminate much subjectivity and decrease the risk that we might use the limited scope of a single leader's mind as a standard.

ONE SIZE DOES NOT FIT ALL

How does the team fit into the science and art of leadership? A problem with many leadership slogans is that they tell us what the goal is without giving specific examples of what needs to be done. For example, the goal is to get the employees to "work as a team focused on excellence and innovation in business." But how exactly do you get people to work as a team toward this goal? Start by doing a *Jack and Jill*. How do you define team? What does it mean to be a team player? What if somebody is a loner? Does this mean that he or she cannot be a productive part of a team? How do you help the team attain and maintain focus? Telling them, "You must focus!" will most certainly not be enough. How do you define excellence? Give some specific examples. What does innovation mean? These words may seem self-explanatory, but are they really? If you fail to define, you will also fail to communicate clearly. When you fail to communicate, it will be difficult to get others to agree. And when you cannot reach agreement, your mission will likely fail. Remember that to get others to agree with the conclusion you must first get them to agree with the premises.

It is also important to understand that you cannot be all to everybody. In other words, do not be a cosmic clause. It is better to stand for something than to stand for everything. When communicating with your employees, ask yourself whether you are honest and avoid communicating values as if they were facts. My guess is that you will say about yourself that you are honest, but consider also how others perceive you. If you are in the habit of looking at the floor whenever you pass somebody in the hallway, the employees may falsely translate your behavior as dishonesty. There is a fitting parable:

> A dog was chasing a rabbit, but when he caught the rabbit he did not know what to do with his prey. First he bit the rabbit, and then he licked the rabbit and wagged his tail. The rabbit said: "What is the meaning with all this? If you do not want to harm me, then why do you bite me? And if you do want

to harm me, then why do you lick me and wag your tail?" Conclusion? It is better with an honest foe than an inconsistent friend. At least you know what you've got.

The team is not for everybody. As politically wrong as it sounds, to maintain pride the team must discriminate; it must include some people while excluding others. If you were a top-rated football player, would you really be happy playing on a team where some of the members were allowed to skip tryouts and practice and play anyway, no matter how lousy they were? Likewise, a top-rated team in the workplace is not a *one-size-fits-all* concept. For those who like to Lead with War, this is the same idea that gives the Marines the right to call themselves "the few, the proud." Pride comes from knowing that you are unique, stronger, and better than the competition. As stated previously, winning matters. Teamwork is not about creating a win-win situation. Rather, the team is zero-sum: We win, you lose. It matters less whose team you are on as long as you are on the winning team. (Remember why we admire Napoleon Bonaparte? Not because he had great character, but because he knew how to win.) If your company is failing, would you feel as proud to work there?

And yes, size matters, too. If the team needs nine members to function and you are number ten, you are the one they do not need. If the team needs ten members to function and you are number ten, you are the piece that makes the puzzle whole. Exactly how many members does the team need? Or is this even an issue? Perhaps it is as simple as saying that bigger is better? Think about it: If everybody works for the same company and toward the same goal, it would seem natural that a big team would have a greater driving force. This hypothetical example does not take cost into consideration. In other words, you do not need to be concerned with whether or not a big team is cost effective at the moment. So if the payroll is not an issue, is bigger still better? If money is not an issue, bigger may sound better. But consider this: When groups are too large, smaller groups tend to form within the larger groups, and as a result everyone on the team will not care about everyone else. You will thus be stuck with the "us vs. them" mentality, which naturally goes against the grain of team building. For empirical evidence, particularly if you work for a large company, you might want to take a peek into the break room on any given day and observe how certain employees always group together and form natural "teams."

Each team member must also be needed and know that the team cannot function without him or her. A team that is too large will have many members with overlapping skills and, therefore, some members will be expendable. As a result each member's importance is reduced. Would it be true to say that the company where you work, which has a branch in almost every state of the Union, is a single team? Or would it be truer to say that the branch in Denver is one team and the branch in New York is another team? If you visit the branch in Denver, would you say that the workers in the five different departments within this branch are on the same team? Or is truer to say that they are on different teams? If your company hires contract workers as part of the workforce, are they on the same team as the regulars or on a different team? If you limit the size of the team, should you treat the members of your particular team the same as the members of another team within your company? Why, or why not? Now let us say that you are in charge of several smaller departments. How would you go about increasing cooperation and teamwork between different departments? What are some of the barriers you might run into regarding support from other teams within your company? When you attempt to break barriers, is there a risk that you are actually creating more barriers? Explain.

At one place of employment there were almost eight hundred workers in a particular building. For many years these workers were split into smaller teams. That is until management came up with the not so brilliant idea that all workers should be grouped together into one large team; throw all names in a hat, so to speak. Why? For cross-utilization and to break barriers, they said. Not wanting to split from their particular team and buddies, the work group protested heavily. But management told them that since there is no "I" in team, it should not matter where they work or with whom. When this concept went into effect, many of the employees stopped caring about the customer. Why? Because grouping everybody together killed their motivation; they no longer felt that they had ownership of their particular department or work area; they were unable to identify with the team. But what about the customer, you may ask? After all, it is not the customer's fault that management killed the workers' motivation and acted so poorly and with so little forethought. Well, yes. However, the team does not work for the customer. Each team member works for the other members on the team. The reason why is because it is the team and not the customer who gives the members their identity. Good customer service is a byproduct of a well-run team. If you want good customer service you must first fix the team. Now with this understood, let us look at the team from a scientific perspective and use a concept from physics to illustrate a principle.

WHO STOLE "I" FROM TEAM?

Molecules are the building blocks of all that exists. They are the smallest units of any substance, and are comprised of clusters of atoms with particular properties. The way the atoms combine determines the type and properties of the molecules. The stronger the bonds between atoms are, the stronger the molecule is. Diamonds, for example, are very hard because the carbon atoms of the diamond are connected by strong chemical bonds. But a molecule can also be as simple as a combination of two like atoms, as is the case with oxygen. Some of the simplest molecules, like oxygen and water, also have the greatest life-sustaining properties. Just as molecules vary in strength and contain a combination of properties, a functional team must be varied and strong and contain a combination of qualities including those that are complex and those that are simple. English physicist Sir Isaac Newton (1642-1727 CE) used a prism to discover that he could split light into the colors of the rainbow, and how all wavelengths of light when mixed formed into a white beam. This observation is analogous to the parts that make up a unit, or what we call the whole. Although each part has different qualities, the particles can blend into a single unit. With this in mind I would like to ask, who stole "I" from team?

"There is no I in team" is one of the most overused and abused team sayings. No matter who you are or where you work you will no doubt remember some sport coach, supervisor, or motivational speaker telling you just this. No doubt will you remember somebody's calendar posted on somebody's office wall displaying this particular slogan. And, yes, it is easy to agree without giving it further thought. After all, who can argue that by definition a team must be comprised of more than one person? Who can argue that it is the team's cohesiveness and ability to work as one that makes it strong, that strength is in numbers, that nobody won a war with a one-man army (if you like to Lead with War), and that if you place your own comfort and well-being ahead of the team, you are likely to get ousted from the team? But without doing a *Jack and Jill*, we have, in fact, gained no more insight than we would have by saying that it is raining, which in and of itself is neither good nor bad. As explored previously, if you are a farmer battling months of drought, you will no doubt be delighted at the rainfall. If you are going on a picnic for your child's tenth birthday, you will most likely be of the opinion that somebody literally "rained on your parade."

The "no I in team" concept refers not to the actual spelling of the word *team*, of course, as this idea would have no relation to leadership or team play whatsoever. However, the assumption is that since there is no "I" in the word *team* (literally), there should be no "I" in the actual teamwork concept either. Is this a good assumption? Is it logic? I do not think so. Why not? Because A does not logically lead to B for the simple reason that grammar and teamwork are not even remotely related. In fact, if you went to a different country, you may well find an "I" in the word for *team* in that country's language. In the pinyin Romanization of Chinese Mandarin, for example, the word for team is *dui*. (Look, there is an "I" in it!) Does this mean that a principle that is true for us Americans is untrue in China? Of course not! The saying is a play on words, nothing more, and if you do a *Jack and Jill*, you will find that the saying cannot automatically be transformed into any particular truths about teamwork. As emphasized in *First, Break All the Rules*, "The point here seems to be that teams are built on collaboration and mutual support. The whole is apparently more important than its individual parts." However, a productive team is "one where each person knows which role he plays best and where he is cast in that role most of the time."[140]

Why should we care about no "I" in team if we do not also have some way of associating ourselves with the deeper meaning of teamwork? The saying is in principle as meaningful (or meaningless) as describing the American flag as thirteen stripes for the original states and fifty stars for the current states. Who cares about the stars and the stripes, if we do not also have some way of associating ourselves with the meaning of our flag?

People *die* for the flag! Why?

People die for the flag because it is a symbol of our identity; it is who we are. Take a look at your company's widget. You have seen it a hundred times. If I asked you to describe it, and all you did was give me the facts: its colors and shapes, then you

137

are missing the boat. A flag, an emblem, and a widget serve to unite a people. You raise the flag and pledge allegiance to it because you identify with it. How you perform has a lot to do with your identity; in other words, how you feel about yourself. Go to the ski-hill, the beach, or the gym and observe how people dress and act. Some people feel "cool" dressing up, others feel cool dressing casual; some people like bright colors, others like earth tones. But we all want to feel cool (or hot, for that matter). If you could dress any way you wanted, what would you wear? If you could drive any car you wanted, what would you drive? Why? When we feel cool about ourselves, we are "in the zone," we are in tune with ourselves. We have an identity. We know who we are. This is the essence of teamwork.

Once you start dissecting the saying, you will begin to see that the idea is more complex than what first meets our ears; that it has implications that extend far beyond the saying itself. The team must function as a unit; this is part of the meaning of no "I" in team. A unit has all its parts so interrelated that it looks like one. In physics, atoms are the building blocks of molecules and form a substance with specific bonds and qualities, such as strength (a diamond) or life (water). The company where you work may be a unit outwardly. You know it because of the company colors and widgets on the equipment and worker uniforms. You know it because of the slogans. Yet a functional team must be both varied and strong. To function as unit, all its parts must be so interrelated that it looks like one. But its strength—and this is important—lies not in the similarities of the many parts that make it up, but in the *differences*. Take a jigsaw puzzle. When completed, it forms a perfect picture, yet no two parts look the same. Each team member holds an intricate piece of the puzzle. If you were building a brick wall you would stagger the bricks for strength. Likewise, a diamond is strong because of the complexity of the bonds between the atoms. How should a team be constructed for strength, then?

If the relationship between the different parts is not honed the unit will fail. If the unit fails, each individual part (team member) will also fail. This is what we mean when we say "one for all—all for one." Simultaneously, and as explored previously, we must understand why it is important who gets the credit. Thus your job as a team leader is not to promote a team that is uniform, but to build a team with complementary qualities. Throughout the rest of your study keep these simple concepts in mind, and when asked what comes first, the team or the individual, remember that although molecules are the building blocks of all that exists, atoms are the building blocks of molecules just as individuals are the building blocks of teams.

Let us look at the "I-chain" inherent to a successfully run team. (With some ingenuity, you might think of plenty more parts to include in this chain.) If you break the chain, you break the strength of the team:

1. Identity
2. Individualism
3. Size
4. Importance
5. Inclusion-Exclusion
6. Pride
7. Intelligence
8. Integrity

A successful team contains **identity**, or the unique need of the individual to be part of the team. Identity is established through team colors, songs, uniforms, slogans, and widgets. **Individualism** is the ability of each member to experience the value he or she brings to the team. Note that although individualism should be encouraged rather than dampened, it must still be managed. There must be certain guidelines, for example, in dress code and safety; there must be some kind of protocol to follow for accomplishing the job in accordance with the company's image. Too much freedom or individualism without staying within the values of the organization results in a loss of identity rather than in a stronger team. It could also jeopardize safety and customer service. Performing according to a set procedure also allows us to transfer what we learn to our peers. If everybody develops their own way of doing things, the "system" becomes un-teachable; we are ignoring the primary thing that makes us human: our ability to transfer knowledge and findings to others without reinventing the wheel. Transferring knowledge through tested and managed procedures helps us accelerate learning and make improvements.

Size is directly related to how well the team can function as a unit. A team that is too large will prevent the members from feeling ownership, and a team that is too small will prevent the members from functioning efficiently. And, of course, it matters who gets the credit; thus, **importance** becomes part of the "I-chain." Importance also leads to **inclusion-exclusion**, which helps maintain **pride**. The team must discriminate by including those individuals who contribute to the strength of the team while excluding freeloaders. Although a great many of us would die for our flag, at what point would we turn around and say that we have sacrificed enough? Although the ideal is something to live, fight, and even die for, our pride needs constant reinforcement to remain a motivating force. And from a competitive standpoint, it does not make sense to include the competition in our team strategies. The team must therefore be exclusive of the competition and of those members whose actions serve to sabotage the cohesiveness of the team. The principle of inclusion-exclusion allows the team members to identify with the team, yet discriminate by understanding the boundaries of the team. A word of caution: Everybody does not have the same ability to work fast or be organized. This is a result of people's differences in age, genetic makeup, etc., and does not automatically mean that those who fall short of your expectations are freeloaders. You must keep individual circumstances and characteristics in mind before criticizing other team members. Ask instead if a person's work really represents his or her best efforts.

Can you use science or statistical data to determine how much work is appropriate for an employee? Can you use scientific evidence to weed out the slackers? Let us say that at the company where you work, some people consistently unload eight freight trucks per day, while others unload only six. If you look at the statistics alone, you might draw the conclusion that those who unload more trucks are the better workers. However, you must also consider that those who unload more trucks have to unload only ten pallets per truck, and not twenty pallets which the supposedly slower workers unload. Now, who are the better workers? Is the person who shoots the most baskets necessarily the best player? Or is he simply selfish by refusing to pass the ball to a team member? By removing the people who unloaded fewer trucks from your workforce, you might actually be removing the keystone of support for your team, and not the slow or lazy workers as you might have thought when you first reviewed the statistics.

Intelligence prevents the leader from misjudging situations that place the team in danger or ridicule. And **integrity** contributes to the cohesiveness of the team. The leader does not own the team physically, mentally, or emotionally. Once everybody understands this, the leader can with good conscience lead his team toward the goal. Think about this: If you need the support of your customers or other "outside people," how would you go about balancing integrity between the customers and your team? At what point do you need to take sides, and whose side should you take? Why? Who should be included and who should be excluded when conflicts arise? How do you create a winning team? You find a leader who uses intelligence and common sense. The leader establishes himself or herself as credible through integrity, or truthfulness and honesty. So, you see, it is easy to babble about "no I in team" and "Together Everybody Achieves More." It is easier to be a yeah-sayer than to think the thought to conclusion.

TEAM VERSUS INDIVIDUAL EXCELLENCE

Marcus Buckingham and Curt Coffman, authors of the highly recommended book, *First, Break All the Rules*, and leaders of The Gallup Organization's effort to identify great workplaces, offer the following insights into team optimization and the value of the individual:

> In the early nineties, one of the leading hospitality companies began experimenting with self-managed work teams as a replacement for the traditional manager role . . . To encourage individual growth, each employee would be able to increase his pay only by learning how to play each of the other roles on the team . . . It was an inspired plan, with only one flaw: It did not work . . . The best housekeepers did not want to become front-desk clerks. They liked housekeeping. Front-desk clerks did not like table serving, and table servers did not appreciate the mess the front-desk clerks were making of their precious restaurant. Each employee came to feel as though he were in the wrong role. He no longer knew exactly what was expected of him. He no longer felt competent, and with the focus on team rather than individual excellence, he no longer felt important.[141]

The study goes on to say: "One team member might occasionally have to step out of his role to support another, but this kind of pinch-hitting should be a rarity on great teams, not their very essence. Whereas conventional wisdom views individual specialization as the antithesis of teamwork, great managers see it as the founding principle."[142]

A word of caution to those who want to optimize teamwork by cross-utilizing employees: According to Webster's Unabridged Dictionary, optimism means that the existing world is the best possible, or "to reach the best outcome in any circumstance." Team optimization is therefore a concept that allows us to reach the

BEST (not just a good) outcome in ANY circumstance (not just on occasion). Cross-utilization does not produce an optimized team. A team that is supposedly optimized through cross-utilization will likely be no team at all. What is supposed to bring the employees together will instead have the opposite effect of sabotaging the team concept. Many employees will no longer know exactly what is expected of them. Many will no longer feel competent, and with the focus on (team) optimization rather than individual excellence, many employees will no longer feel validated or important. Loss of pride will follow, with a subsequent loss in customer service. As a leader in a world class company, is this really what you want?

The reason why people excel is because they have had the opportunity to fine tune and perfect their skills in one specific area. When selecting your team, it is better to look for varied abilities between the people than for varied abilities within the same person. When you have hired your people to perform a specific job and suddenly ask them to do another job or take on additional duties not in their job description, the reason why you run into difficulties may be related to the fact that the people you hired are specialists in their specific areas, and asking them to do other jobs actually means that you are trying to capitalize on their weaknesses and not on their strengths.

The Gallup Organization has also put together a list of questions intended to measure the strength of a workplace and the core elements needed to attract, focus, and keep the most talented employees. This list is a result of the findings from interviews conducted with hundreds of companies, managers, and employees.[143] As an employee evaluating the strength of your workplace, you should strive for as many "yes" answers as possible. Then, to think the thought to conclusion, give an example that supports your answer.

1. Do I know what is expected of me at work?

2. Do I have the materials and equipment I need to do my work right?

3. At work, do I have the opportunity to do what I do best every day?

4. In the last seven days, have I received recognition or praise for doing good work?

5. Does my supervisor, or someone at work, seem to care about me as a person?

6. Is there someone at work who encourages my development?

7. At work, do my opinions seem to count?

8. Does the mission/purpose of my company make me feel my job is important?

9. Are my co-workers committed to doing quality work?

10. Do I have a best friend at work?

11. In the last six months, has someone at work talked to me about my progress?

12. This last year, have I had opportunities at work to learn and grow?

Let us take a moment and explore question 10: Do I have a best friend at work? Having a best friend at work makes you look forward to coming to work. However, one may wonder what a best friend has got to do with teamwork, or how the team leader is supposed to have control over this issue? Here is the problem: If an employee has a best friend at work, but the team leader prevents the employee from working together with his or her friend whenever possible, the many good qualities that go along with friendship, such as a feeling of joy and looking forward to coming to work, are sabotaged. This is one of the core concepts of a cohesive team: The team members must WANT to form a team; a team is not just ANY group of people. People who like each other and want to work together should therefore be placed together.

Efficient teamwork is about developing the qualities you find in each team member, and not trying to make each member what he or she is not. When the employees at one particular corporation desired a change in work habits and delivered a petition to the manager, he rebutted by explaining that a petition "is not our way." But who is the judge? Who determines whose "way" it is when tens of thousands of men and women are employed at this corporation? Who is to say what is safer, more fun, or provides better opportunities? Why is it not only difficult but a bad idea to be the judge for others by defining their objectives for them? It might be wise now to consider the nearly two-thousand year old insights of Petronius Arbiter (c. 27-66 CE), a Roman courtier:

> We trained hard . . . but it seemed that every time we were beginning to form up into teams, we would be reorganized. I was to learn later in life that we tend to meet any new situation by reorganizing; and a wonderful method it can be for creating the illusion of progress while producing confusion, inefficiency, and demoralization.[144]

To reemphasize, you cannot throw together any number of employees and call it a team. The reason why a large team has a greater potential to be a motivation killer than a small team, is because each member on a large team tends to become only a number. In other words, individual identity is lost. Another problem with a large team is that each member will also be shielded from pain and the effects of wrongdoing. Specific responsibilities cannot be delegated because we assume that "it is everybody's responsibility," and, as discussed previously, everybody's responsibility becomes nobody's responsibility. So what exactly is the proper size of the team? This is a difficult question to answer, which is yet a reason why science, which deals with precise numbers and concepts, often cannot be used successfully when dealing with people. However, a good guideline when contemplating team size is to start by defining the tasks the team needs to accomplish and the number of members needed for each task. Then strive to make the team small enough to make no member expendable, and specific enough to bring about feelings of ownership and pride.

Now that you have pondered the previous material, if you still prefer to Lead with Science, here are some scientific terms that might give you a good start.[145] As you consider each term and how it might relate to team leadership, make sure you also do a *Jack and Jill* to detect potential pitfalls.

WAYS TO LEAD WITH SCIENCE

Science is about discovering evidence and relationships for observable phenomena, and establishing theories that organize and make sense of those phenomena. **Technology** is about the tools, techniques, and procedures we use for implementing the scientific findings. If we know the principles but do not have the capacity to utilize them, we are not very successful as leaders. The opposite is also true. If we apply the technology, the methods and techniques, but do not understand the underlying principles, we may end up using the wrong tools and will be unable to perform the job satisfactorily. The **scientific method** is a good place to start, because it organizes our thoughts in the proper sequence and decreases the risk of making mistakes. There are a number of steps that must be followed: Recognize that there is a problem, make an educated guess and predict the consequences (form a hypothesis), perform experiments to test the predictions, and formulate the simplest general rule that organizes the hypothesis and experimental outcome into a theory.

The scientific method thus helps us establish a procedure for finding the facts about a particular issue. What is a fact? A **fact** is a close agreement between competent observers of a series of observations of the same phenomenon. As previously noted, the observers must be *competent*. Depending on their background and competence, the opinions or findings of one person might carry greater weight than the opinions and findings of another. When related to team leadership, the employee is probably the person with the greatest competence when it comes to determining whether or not he or she should embrace a particular change. This is not the same as saying that the employee is qualified to determine, for example, whether or not cutbacks in personnel are necessary to make the company profitable; only that the employee is the authority on whether or not he will embrace or resist cutbacks in personnel. If the leadership tells an employee that he should go to the fish market in Seattle to learn about positive attitudes at work because it is so much fun, but the employee's idea of fun differs from management's, who is the better judge? Who is the more competent "observer"? Who has the fact? The employee is the more competent observer, because he or she alone determines what fun means to him or her in particular.

A **hypothesis**, on the other hand, is an educated guess; a reasonable explanation of an observation of experimental results that is not fully accepted as factual, but that can be used to guide us toward a fact. Before we can establish a new law in science, or a new policy in the workplace, we must form a hypothesis. The problem is that we often tend to jump to conclusions based on the hypothesis without doing sufficient experimentation. Or, worse, we might skip the hypothesis altogether and proceed with a change without even considering, or guessing, how the workforce will react. **Elasticity**, for example, is the ability to change shape when a force is applied and return to the original shape when the force is removed. In teamwork elasticity can be related to flexibility. How many times have you heard that you must be flexible and bend with the forces if you want to realize success? The question of importance is how far a material can be stretched without permanent distortion, or how far a team can be stretched or asked to change before losing motivation and refusing to spring back to its optimum shape.

Hooke's Law states that the extension of an elastic object is directly proportional to the stretching force applied. The **elastic limit** is the distance beyond which permanent distortion occurs. In leadership it is important to have a good sense of the location of this limit or breaking point. Simultaneously keep in mind that an inelastic object, or a team that resists change, tends to be more fragile and break more easily than an elastic object and must therefore be treated more delicately if you want to avoid sabotaging the positive qualities of the team. **Pressure**, by contrast, is the ratio of force to the area over which that force is distributed. When you apply a large force to a small area you will exert a lot of pressure, and vice versa. You must therefore have a fine sense of how much pressure your team can handle before it stops functioning properly. You must similarly decide how to distribute that pressure so that it does not fall on just a few members of the team. You can think of pressure in terms of workload. How many employees do you need to hire to reach maximum efficiency at minimum cost? How do you handle those who are ambitious versus those who are lazy? Do you put more pressure on the ambitious employees and less on the lazy, or vice versa? Why?

Furthermore, to answer the question of how far a team can be stretched or asked to change before losing motivation and refusing to spring back to its optimum shape, we must understand something about teams, their composition and how the individual parts interact with one another. In physics, **molecules** are tiny parts that make up living as well as non-living things. The more complex the molecular pattern the stronger the object. A team can be viewed as a complex organism where total strength rests in the differences and not similarities between individuals. However, exactly how a team should look to achieve its goal, or what type of "molecule" will be most beneficial, must also be determined. Although complex makes strong, some of the simplest molecules like water and oxygen are also the most life sustaining. So just how complex should your team be? How inclusive should it be of new team members? Remember that when bringing new members in, the "atoms" that build the molecules must rearrange and you will get a **chemical reaction** which could manifest as a violent explosion.

A **change of state** in the molecular structure can also occur when heat is absorbed, which causes the molecules to vibrate more and more violently. When enough heat is absorbed the attractive forces between the molecules will no longer hold them together. Bonds will break. Think about how this applies to teamwork. When the bonds between individuals break due to too much "steam" within the team, the group will become unstable and unable to function as a unit. Steam has even more potential energy than boiling water, because the molecules are relatively free to move about and even a slight disturbance will set them off. By contrast, if too little heat is applied, all energy is withdrawn and the group will lose motivation and become lethargic. One way to use this concept when Leading with Science is to relate it to motivation. How do you find the correct balance between the gung-ho leader (or team) and the pacifist who does not seem to care much one way or the other?

To keep a constant flow of energy you must consistently apply pressure, but not so much that it breaks the bonds between team members and destroys unity. The phenomenon of melting under pressure and freezing again when the pressure is reduced is called **regelation**, and can be applied to the employee's relation to supervision and management. The employee may be more likely to comply with requests when there is pressure to do so. But when the pressure is removed or the supervisor is not looking, the employee will return to the old behavior.

As discussed previously, a fully functioning team must have members with complementary qualities. **Complementary** means "mutually exclusive." Think of this as the yin-yang symbol. Only the union of yin-yang forms a whole. With respect to leadership, this concept can be likened to how one part, branch, or department of a company cannot function without another. The company cannot function without the customers; management cannot function without the workers, and vice versa. The customer is not always right, but neither is the company. The boss is not always right, but neither is the employee. Each group must complement the others to form a whole, or what we call a workable and efficient team.

With respect to determining the proper size of the team for optimum unit cohesion, we can consider **vector quantities** that have both magnitude and direction. It is not only important how big something is, but also in what direction it is moving. We might want to remember that as the size of an object increases, the object grows heavier much faster than it grows stronger. This is called **scaling**. Thus bigger does not necessarily translate into stronger, which is why it is crucial to understand that a team has an optimum size that allows it to function as a unit where members can bond properly and avoid wasting energy. Cohesion, of course, is an important team concept. In physics, **cohesion** is the attraction between like substances, and **adhesion** is the attraction between unlike substances. Perhaps it is adhesion rather than cohesion that should be considered when building a team. As explored earlier, a team with too many similar qualities between its members will be less strong than a team with unlike but complementary qualities.

Once you have established a proper composition for your team, the next step is to put it to work. **Energy** is defined as anything that can change the condition of matter or has the ability to do work. Conservation of energy and the **First Law of Thermodynamics** states that energy output can never exceed energy input. If many years pass where there is no inflow of energy, or no motivation, the workforce will become lethargic. By contrast, when you add energy to a system such as a team, it can convert that energy to a different form and produce work that helps the company achieve the desired goals. The **Second Law of Thermodynamics** states that heat will never flow by itself from a cold object to a hot object. Heat (like the proverbial shit) flows only one way: downhill from hot to cold. This is why, when the supervisor takes "heat" from his superiors, the employees will surely take heat from the supervisor in the near future. We can also think of this as "passing the buck." Unfortunately, the buck is normally passed in a negative sense.

Natural systems further tend to proceed toward a state of greater disorder or randomness, producing a lot of waste. Disordered energy can be changed to ordered energy only at the expense of some organizational effort. **Entropy** is the measure of the amount of disorder. Whenever a physical system is allowed to distribute its energy freely, entropy generally increases, resulting in a decrease in ability of the available energy to do work. This is why we need leadership. When entropy occurs, there must be an input of energy to restore the strength of the original system. When a team is allowed to break apart, it takes more energy to restore it to its original shape than the amount of energy that was lost through entropy. This is why first impressions are important and why it is difficult to remedy a leadership faux pas. Every change you implement that is perceived by the team in negative terms will create a slight loss from the "original." Liken this to using a copy machine. The copy will never be of the same quality as the original, and the more copies you make of each new copy, the worse they will appear. No machine can be completely efficient in converting energy to work, and all systems tend to become more and more disorganized as time goes by. If not managed, organized systems will eventually decay and descend into chaos; that is unless the system is open and allows for proper transfer of energy.

If energy can change the condition of matter and has the ability to do work, then what is work? **Work** is the force times the distance, and **power** is the work done over a particular time interval. If you can move an object over a short distance, little work is required for a given force. If you can move an object in a short time, you have a lot of power. But since energy is what enables you to do work, if you want to do a lot of work you must think of a way to conserve energy (perhaps by working smarter and not harder). No machine or device can put out more energy than is put into it. Although it can multiply force, it cannot multiply energy. How **efficient** something is can be expressed by the ratio of work done over energy used. Thus if you are very efficient, you can do a lot of work without expending a lot of energy. If you expend a lot of energy, you ought to rethink how you do the work. When there is inefficiency much energy is wasted. Work that does not lead to results is a waste of energy. A prime example is what is popularly referred to as "busy work," delegated to employees when management does not like them sitting idle. Busy work does not make a company more efficient. Busy work and inefficiency in general also tends to have a negative effect on employee pride and motivation; it tends to destroy the team's momentum.

Momentum means inertia in motion, and **inertia** means resistance to change. The faster an object moves and the heavier it is, the more difficult it is to stop its motion or reverse its direction. As we have discussed repeatedly throughout this study, people resist change; it is a natural quality that is not easily overcome. When you try to implement change, there *will* be inertia. Implementing change in the workplace is particularly difficult when you need to convince a large group of people of your views, particularly if these people are already opposed to your views. You must not only stop their current motion which is directing them away from your views, you must also start motion in a new direction. Change in direction means a change in momentum because a component part of the momentum equation is **velocity**, or speed and direction. An alternative to stopping the motion or slowing it down when desiring to change the momentum is to change the direction through the application of an outside force.

Impulse is another way to look at the change in momentum. A large change in momentum in a short time requires a large force. Thus implementing a sudden rather than gradual change will require a large force. **Forces**, whether small or large, always occur in pairs with each force acting in the opposite direction of the other. Or, according to **Newton's Third Law of Motion**, to every action, there is an equal and opposite reaction. So when you exert a force in the workplace, you create an *interaction* between yourself and the person against whom you exert the force. It is thus unreasonable to exert a force against a person without also expecting to feel the effects of that force. **Friction** is a force resisting motion. Since it takes energy to overcome friction, you should evaluate beforehand how much friction the change in a procedure is likely to cause among the employees, and whether or not it will be worth the effort. Friction always acts in a direction opposing motion. Moreover, **irregularities** act as obstructions to motion. When we fail to agree on issues, we have irregularities and therefore friction. When implementing a change that your employees resist, to overcome friction you must first apply a force that is equal to the force of friction just to reach neutral ground. When this has been done, you must apply an additional force to get the employees moving in the new direction. Change can therefore be tremendously energy consuming and troublesome. If possible you want to start negotiations for change from a position of minimal friction between your views and those of the employees.

You must also be aware of a possible **chain reaction**, or a self-sustaining reaction that once started steadily provides the energy and matter necessary to continue the reaction. A chain reaction can provide a great effect through little energy. Before starting an action (a change in policy, for example), you must therefore look at the possible consequences and the probability that the action will turn into a chain reaction. Negative information can be intensified through a chain reaction, and if you are not careful have undesirable consequences that will spiral out of control. Furthermore, when different substances rub against or touch one another there is a **charge by contact**. By contrast, **charging by induction** is the redistribution of charges in and on objects caused by the electrical influence of an object nearby but not in contact. When using this idea in the workplace, you can feel the effects of another person's mood or behavior even if he or she is not directing the behavior toward you in particular. Rather, the atmosphere around this person gets "charged," either positively or negatively.

Do waves within the team make it stronger or weaker? Wave motion can tell you something about the source that is producing the wave. A **wave** is the transfer of energy from a source to a distance receiver without the transfer of actual matter between the two points. As mentioned previously, if a rock is dropped into a pond waves will travel outward in expanding circles. But if the wave experiences an obstacle such as a concrete wall, the water will run back into the pond and things will be much as they were before the initial disturbance. Although the water in the pond was disturbed it did not go anywhere or accomplish anything, and the medium returned to its original condition after the disturbance had ceased. With respect to leadership we can think of the transfer of information within an organization in terms of waves. Or we can think of waves as the transfer of energy from one employee to another. When energy is transferred between employees, the group as a whole may be motivated to perform a task.

In physics, the speed of the wave is equal to its frequency times the wavelength. A short wavelength translates into a high frequency or a more violent disturbance, and vice versa. Moreover, a single location is not limited to one vibration or wave. Also, as discussed previously, if you drop two rocks into water, the waves produced by each can overlap and form an interference pattern. Within this pattern wave effects may be increased, decreased, or neutralized. Waves may be reinforced in some places and cancelled in others by this interference pattern. When the crest of one wave overlaps the crest of another their individual effects are summarized, called **constructive interference**. With respect to team leadership we can say that the two waves have in effect team worked to produce an overall stronger wave. However, be aware that the term constructive can be misleading. Increasing the overall effect of the wave does not necessarily mean that you achieve an overall more positive outcome. **Destructive interference**, where you calm the effect and flatten the wave, may in fact be more "constructive" in a work environment. Consider also that the expression "making waves" is generally used in a negative sense.

Thus whether it is better to make waves or calm waves depends on what you are trying to achieve. Let us look at **sound waves.** Is sound objective or subjective? Or as the cliché goes: If a tree falls in the forest and nobody is there to hear it, will it make a sound? If you hold a briefing and nobody is there to hear you, does your speech have meaning? The transmission of sound requires a medium, because if there is nothing to compress and expand there can be no sound. Let us say that you have an audience, but they do not *want* to listen. So they hear only what they want to hear and not what is actually being said. This is a communication problem. The so-called grapevine is an example of how sound travels like a wave even to those who did not hear the original speaker. The reflection of sound is called an **echo**. If the surfaces reflecting the sound are too reflective, however, the sound becomes garbled and induces multiple reflections called **reverberations**. When this happens you may not hear the sound as it was originally intended. This is what propagates the transmission of rumors.

Mirrors are poor **absorbers** but good **reflectors**. Rough surfaces are better absorbers but poorer reflectors. It is difficult to be a good absorber and a good reflector at the same time. This concept, too, can be related to communication. Although you can be both a good transmitter and a good receiver of information by thinking about what you want to say before you say it, and ensuring that you really listen to what is being said when your team comes to you with their concerns, you cannot be a good transmitter and a good receiver precisely at the same time. It is only possible to focus on one issue at a time whether transmitting or receiving. Likewise, multi-tasking which has become increasingly popular, is an idea that should be rethought. Are employees really more efficient when they are forced to focus on several issues simultaneously? Might it be better if they were allowed to finish one task before being asked to perform another?

Consider also how aberration affects communication. In physics, **aberration** is the distortion of an image produced by a lens or system of lenses. No lens provides a perfect image. Aberration can be minimized by combining lenses in certain ways.

For this reason most optical instruments use compound lenses, each consisting of several simple lenses instead of a single lens. In the workplace, if you want a clear and truthful view of your policies, you must involve others and ask for their views (you must look at the situation through different lenses), because your view alone may be distorted by a number of factors. This concept relates to **parallax**, or the apparent change in position of an object resulting from a change in the viewer's position. Due to the error of the parallax, what you see from your position may not be what is actually there. To get a true image, objects must be viewed from a true position. If you view your team's performance from the outside but do not really experience it firsthand, your opinion of what is happening may be invalid simply because of your position. This can also be thought of as **frame of reference**, or a vantage point with respect to which an object may be described. Depending on where you stand, your frame of reference will differ from somebody else's. A team leader or manager, for example, may not see what the employees see because he is literally not in the fray on a daily basis and may therefore make false assumptions about the work environment.

WHAT DO YOU OWE YOUR TEAM?

Now that you have gained an understanding of ways to Lead with Science, the strengths and the pitfalls, ask yourself what you really owe your team and what your team owes you outside of what is stated in your written contract. Or do you owe each other nothing but eight hours of work and a paycheck? When you evaluate your team members, what do you wish to achieve and how will you use the evaluations to further your goals? Is your purpose to inspire employees to become more efficient? Although motivation may be our strongest driving force, to remain hungry and receptive to motivation the employee must realize the value of the task he or she is attempting to accomplish. In other words, the evaluation must make him or her feel good about working. The work must matter, the results must matter, and they must matter in the near future. If "above standard" on an evaluation promises a pay raise five years from now, it will most likely not serve as a good motivator. Likewise, "[w]aiting to praise or reprimand an employee for a specific behavior at a semi-annual performance review . . . will have a marginal impact on performance . . . [Y]early performance appraisals, annual recognition dinners, quarterly bonuses, and employee of the month contests have little or no impact on organizational performance."[146]

Rewards must also be large enough to make a difference. They must be fair. A year-end bonus that is given only to those who have worked for the company at least ten years will create negative attitudes for those who worked just as hard in the last year but only have three years of service with the company. Which is fair: Should a bonus be a percentage of your salary, or should it be equal for everybody? This and other questions must be answered and considered carefully before proceeding. The consequences of your actions must also be considered, and whether they will help or hinder the situation.

CONSTRUCTIVE CRITICISM? OH YEAH?!

Critique increases motivation, *but only* if the critique is fair and the person critiqued understands its value. For the record, a critique is "a critical and unbiased analysis," which is not the same as *criticism*. Know the difference. You can give constructive critique but not constructive criticism. Criticism is by nature destructive. Although critique may be unpleasant and invite the possibility of an attack on your person, when allowed to critique widely we eliminate much subjective thought. When critiquing an employee's performance, for the critique to have meaning you must first ensure that the employee welcomes your input and is in a position to receive it. If you think you can change a person or a person's behavior without his or her approval, place yourself in the position of the person critiqued and the answer will immediately become clear. Furthermore, for a critique to be valid it must account for the verified results of a former critique; it must *correspond* with the former critique.

Here is an example: Joe's annual evaluation is due. The company has printed forms for this purpose, and you check the appropriate boxes for below standard, standard, and above standard performance for the different work duties. You call Joe into the office, give him a copy of the evaluation, and ask him to read and sign it. But Joe is unhappy despite the fact that you have given him mostly high marks. You have the sense to ask why, and Joe explains that this year's evaluation does not correspond with last year's evaluation. Last year another supervisor evaluated Joe, and Joe now wants to know why you evaluated him as standard on ability to work with others, when the other supervisor gave him an above standard score in this particular area. You tell Joe that you have never had any complaints about him from his peers, but nobody in particular has complimented him either so you feel the standard mark fits. But Joe is still not happy and explains that last year nobody complained or complimented him either, yet the work went smoothly and he received an above standard on the evaluation. You admit that you have not looked at last year's evaluation, and that this year's evaluation is based on your experiences and not on the old boss' experiences. Joe is still unhappy. He is now telling you that an evaluation should not be subjective. If it is only up to your opinion, he says, it has little value because another leader will most certainly have a different opinion. And how can Joe make improvements to his performance if it is based on subjective opinion and not on objective fact?

How do you tackle this problem? You can start by asking whether the results of last year's evaluation have been fully verified, and how. What criteria did the last person use who evaluated Joe? If the criteria have changed or are subjective, will the old evaluation still be valid? Why, or why not? If the old and the new evaluations fail to correspond in the region where the results of the old evaluation have been fully verified, the old evaluation is invalid, the new evaluation is invalid, or both the old and the new evaluations are invalid. An evaluation that is invalid fails to accomplish its intent and is a waste of time.

As Joe noted, an evaluation must also be objective. What is objective? First, it should not be based on personal opinion of performance. In other words, if somebody else had made the same observations of a particular employee's performance he should have given a similar critique. Second, it should not be based on whether or not you, the person administering the critique, like the person you are critiquing. Your mood on the particular day should not interfere. If you give the critique tomorrow, it should be the same as if you give it today. You must also base the critique on the actual performance that took place and not on what could have been. Third, the critique must be flexible to the degree that it fits the particular person, times, and circumstances that you are critiquing. It should not be taken out of context. Fourth, if the person receiving the critique does not agree, or at least accept it, it is worthless. A critique should not be an opportunity to voice your dissatisfaction with the person you are critiquing. For the employee to accept the critique, it is essential that the person administering the critique is an authority on the subject. If the person critiqued does not believe that you know what you are talking about the critique will have little meaning. The fact that you are wearing a team leader patch does not alone qualify you to give an effective and acceptable critique.

Furthermore, a critique does not need to include every single area of performance. Rather, choose one or two points that are current at the moment. Remember to include the positive aspects of the employee's performance and not just the areas that need improvement. Finally, if the critique does not serve the intended purpose: to profit the person receiving the critique, it has failed. The person critiqued must thus know how to capitalize on the things covered in the critique. When identifying strengths and weaknesses you must also provide a satisfactory explanation of how you reached your assessment. When identifying weaknesses you must provide a specific way to overcome them. Disciplinary action, like critique, is useless unless it leads you a step closer to your objective. If you need to discipline a worker, how can you ensure that the discipline is constructive and more than a way for you to vent your feelings? How do you tailor it to benefit the needs of your organization?

THE END OR THE MEANS?

The end is more important than the means, at least at a civilian place of employment. This is one reason why it is counterproductive to evaluate a person on whether or not he or she used the customer's name in conversation, smiled at the customer, or finished the conversation with, "Thank you for calling (enter your company's name here)." If whatever the employee did resulted in customer satisfaction, then exactly what he did is important only to him and not to the supervisor or others, because if they were to do the exact same thing it may not prove as effective because it would not play to their natural talents. When following a predetermined script such as, "Thank you for calling . . ." or, "How may I help you?" or using the customer's name at least twice, or making at least three attempts to sell a product, we tend not to hear the customer anymore but become absorbed only in following the script for fear that we may be monitored and *criticized.* This kind of monitoring and criticism is meaningless and misses the point, because the employee would be evaluated on how well he or she follows the script and not on how well he or she treats the customer. He would thus be evaluated on the means and not the end.

One company recently implemented a quality assurance program which required team leaders to observe and evaluate the employees during their performance. One leader confessed that he had to evaluate each employee twice during the month and had more than fifty employees to evaluate. First, if you have to produce a forced evaluation this often it is an indication that you do not know the people on your team. And if you do not know your people, you are not fit to be their leader. Second, just about all of the employees were receiving high marks in all areas but were offered little specific input. In other words, the team leader wrote the evaluation only because there was pressure from above and not because he considered it an important part of the operation. If you are a team leader evaluating or rating an employee and you cannot offer specific input, it may be tempting to use an "average" rating. Try to avoid this temptation. Do not rate on a scale from one to five, for example, because it would tempt you to choose "three."

The idea is that we are either happy or not. Choosing the average score is a copout. You are in fact saying that you are not completely happy with the employee, but you are not unhappy either. In other words, you can get by with the status quo, which means that there is really no motivation to improve. So what do we do? We get by.

The end is thus more important than the means, because the means must always be judged in relation to the end they serve. If the end is not achieved, the procedure of going through an evaluation process is useless. Before implementing a quality assurance program you must first define the end objective: What are you trying to achieve? If you are trying to achieve better workers (whatever that means) but the evaluation serves to antagonize the workers, then you have not achieved the end objective. If the workers accept the evaluation but do not change as a result, you have not achieved the end objective. To reiterate: For people to change, they must want to change. How do you know if you will reach the end objective before you have wasted your time? A good place to start is by asking those affected: the workers. If they take negatively to your ideas, you might want to proceed cautiously

EVALUATING THE LEADER

Just as an evaluation done by the team leader must be precise with clearly defined objectives to have meaning, so must an evaluation done by the employees. When I asked my coworkers what qualities they would like to see in a team leader, their answers were weighted toward following through on commitments and promises, offering help even if no help is needed, and asking for opinions before implementing new rules. As an employee, if you are offered a questionnaire about how the leadership is doing, simply checking a box that says that the manager recognizes excellence tells us nothing of value about the leadership. You need to take it a step further and ask *how*. Then give a specific example. If you cannot give a specific example of how the team leader stresses teamwork or holds people accountable for their actions, he or she will fail to identify with the critique and the critique will be meaningless; it will be nothing but an exercise in futility and a waste of time.

By contrast, a well conducted team leader/manager evaluation done by the employees will give the leadership the ability to extract information that can be used to make the company more productive. To act on the information the team leaders must also have their manager's blessing; they must be allowed to do the job that has been delegated to them. To score well on an evaluation as a team leader, you must understand and have insight into the following:

1. **For whom you are working.** There is only one correct answer. I will give you a hint: It is in your title. The team leader is serving the team. You are not serving the customer, the company, or the manager. You are serving the team. Period. In other words, if you answer that you are working for the company, the team, management, your paycheck, and the customer, it would be a cosmic clause statement that dilutes the role of the leader and indicates that you do not have a clear understanding of what it means to be a team leader. Choose one of the above, not all. The team leader does not wear many hats, as some would have us believe. The team leader has only one responsibility: his team. It is

thus important that you understand your role. Being a leader is not a prerequisite for becoming a manager or a business executive. Some would have us believe that it is, but there is really very little practical connection. The reverse is also true. Team leaders and company managers play distinctly different roles. This concept holds true for many jobs within the company. There is not necessarily a "ladder" within the team or company that each employee must climb. The duties that need to be performed require different talents, and one job function does not naturally lead to another. (Must a pilot be a flight attendant before he or she can be a pilot? Must an author write children's books before he or she can write for adults? Of course not. The occupations are different and one is not a steppingstone for the other.) Some individuals are, of course, good at performing several functions, but it should not be assumed that everybody can be trained to do so successfully or is interested in being trained for a new position for that matter. An outstanding leader must also do more than what is naturally expected of him. If the company places a slogan on the wall that reads, "What have you done today that made the customer smile?" answer this question as a leader: "What have you done today that made an employee smile?" Be specific. Simply saying that you are fair and listen to suggestions coming from your team is not precise enough. Additionally, just as airline customers expect to be delivered to their destination safely, being fair and listening to suggestions sort of comes with your position and does not add any additional value to your score.

2. **For whom your team is working.** Again, there is only one correct answer. I will give you a hint: Your team (if it is well-run and efficient) does NOT work for the team leader, the company, or the customer. All of these answers are wrong. The team is serving itself. Customer service is a byproduct of a well-run team. This concept lies at the heart of team leadership. When you select your team, you must select people who want to work with each other. As already explored, randomly grouping any number of people together does not make a team. When people want to work together, they will help each other and further contribute to the cohesiveness of the team. Without team

cohesiveness you do not have a team; each worker will be working alone. As a result customer service will suffer.

3. **The misuse and abuse of the saying, "there is no I in team."** As we have already explored, the team is built around the "I" concept. Identity, for example, involves more than wearing the uniform or mouthing a slogan. The "selfish" needs of the team members must be satisfied before the needs of the customer can be satisfied. Feed the team first to establish a sense of pride and ownership. The members of the team must feel their successes regularly and know that their opinions matter. The team's vision must also be stated clearly, agreed upon by the members, and achievable within a reasonable time. "To become the world's greatest" is in a practical sense as useless as "to become a millionaire" or "to understand the meaning of life." Remember that your team could do a better job IF they wanted to. The trick is not making them do a better job, but identifying the factors that will make them WANT to do a better job.

Furthermore, the leader should be an ally and not a troublemaker. Perceived dishonesty is just as bad as true dishonesty. At one corporation, one of the leaders revealed that he had received only two out of five possible points for honesty on an evaluation done by the workers, and it puzzled him. At the same corporation, one of the managers realized that he must work on improving the relationship between the team and the leadership. It took him forty-five minutes to walk from one end of the hallway to the other because he could not take a step without being stopped by frustrated workers whose team leaders had failed to follow up on their concerns.

There is little incentive for employees to be committed to the goals of an organization that makes no reciprocal commitment to the employees. Getting out of the office and mingling with the employees can be a simple solution to common trust problems. However, one must also ensure that the employees understand the reason for the manager or team leader getting out of the office. If he appears out of character by doing so, he risks losing trust rather than gaining it. Do a *Jack and Jill*: How should the manager or team leader be visible? In the shadows? In the break room? In the work area? Why? Where should he not be? Employees with customer contact are often told that they are in a fishbowl; that they should be aware of their behavior because the customers are constantly watching. This idea applies also to the leader. The difference is that he is on stage for those he leads. Every move you make is observed and evaluated by your employees and contributes to the attitudes they form about you and the job.

When striving to score well on an evaluation done by the employees the leader should keep in mind that:

1. Most people do not like change, never have, and never will. This is the truth! Forcing change when not warranted ALWAYS has a negative outcome.

2. Most people respond much better if you ask them what they want rather than tell them what they should want.

3. Most people are not lazy and do not inherently dislike work. But just as a successful marriage requires constant reinforcement, so does a successful team leader/team relationship

Now, then, it is the employee's turn. If you are an employee, here are some suggestions that might help you answer questions that might appear on an evaluation you are asked to write about your team leader's performance. If you cannot answer all of these questions by giving specific examples, you need to slow down, backtrack, or take a good look at the full picture and question whether your assumptions are really valid.

MY TEAM LEADER

1. **Cares about whether or not I am happy at work and makes an effort to find out what makes me tick.** When you answer this question, rather than simply placing an X in the "yes" or "no" box, state what your team leader has done to indicate that he cares about your satisfaction. For example, has he or she recently asked what you need to feel job satisfaction? If he or she does not care about you, you will feel as though you are just a number among others without specific value. When you have no value, you will not put forth the effort to do a good job.

2. **Asks my opinion about issues that affect me and makes an attempt to accommodate my views.** Has your supervisor asked your opinion regarding issues that affect you; for example, with whom you would like to work, in which area you would like to work (if applicable), whether you have the equipment you need to do your job efficiently, and what in particular can be done to make you feel more joy about coming to work? How important is it that he or she implements your suggestions? Or is it good enough if the leader says, "Yes, I hear you and I agree, but there is nothing I can do about it!" A leader must work for his people's cause. If the arguments presented by the employees are not valid, they still need to be discussed until the leader and the employees reach common ground.

3. **Acknowledges my efforts and rewards me for my work when warranted.** When answering this question, keep in mind that proper recognition generally involves more than a "good job yesterday." There must be some form of concrete reward. For example, if employee A finishes a job faster than employee B, then employee A should be personally rewarded (for example, with a break), and not "punished" by being asked to work more than employee B, in which case the supervisor would in effect be rewarding the slackers.

4. **Gives suggestions for how I might improve my performance.** As discussed previously, for feedback to be

constructive problems must first be agreed upon between team leader and employee. If the supervisor were required to wear a shirt at work with a sign on the back that read, "How is my leadership? Call 1-800- . . ." would he think it a good idea? Even if he or she possesses many good leadership qualities, my guess is that he would not welcome this idea because there is always somebody who is having a bad day and cannot wait to take advantage of the opportunity. For an evaluation to be constructive, both parties involved must agree on the problem area and be allowed to confront each other and discuss it. Anonymous evaluations where the subject has no way of elaborating, asking for clarification, defending himself, etc. will never go over well with the person evaluated, and are in principle always wrong even if the results of the evaluation turn out to be outstanding.

5. **Is available when I need him or her.** There are two sides to consider here: A team leader who gets involved where he is not needed is worse than one who does not get involved at all. A team leader who is visible in the operation does not necessarily ensure that the employees' needs are met.

6. **Has character and creates an impression of integrity and trust.** Many team leaders likely perform their jobs with integrity; they are basically good people. However, do they have the education and drive to be good leaders and not just good people? You may trust your team leader as far as "yes, I feel safe coming to work." But do you trust him or her as far as "will he or she stand up for me if I make a mistake?"

7. **Enforces compliance with established procedures.** Sometimes leaders break the rules, just like employees do when they think they can get away with it and when it helps make their jobs easier. If this happens often consider whether it might be the rules that need an overhaul and not the team leaders. If this is the case, is the team leader willing to rewrite the rules so that they affect everybody equally?

8. Encourages new ideas and is willing to change when applicable. As we have seen, change is not necessarily beneficial and is therefore not necessarily something that should be encouraged. In fact, unneeded change creates stress and sabotages team spirit and work ethics. The team leader will be more successful if he or she asks the employees directly what would help them do a better job. Sometimes we feel there is an artificial need to change. In other words, the need is not real. But since things are not going well, we need to do something about it so that we can prove to our superiors that we have at least addressed the issue. Before implementing the change, did the team leader clearly state why the change was needed and did he or she evaluate it afterward to determine to what extent the change helped fix the problem? A manager at one company admitted to me in private that he forced an unwelcome change that did not improve efficiency, because he had to demonstrate to his superiors that he had made an attempt to improve efficiency or face demotion.

As an alternative when evaluating your team leader, focus only on one issue rather than several and explain how the leader excels or fails on this particular issue. Although we would like to think that the leader should be assertive, friendly, a good listener, flexible, and knowledgeable all at once, does he really need to know every aspect of the operation? Is well-rounded always better than specialist? Why, or why not? Although the team as a whole should have the capacity to perform the entire job, each individual on the team does not need this capacity. Similarly, the leader can be specialized in a particular area of the operation and rely on the support of the team in areas where he is not a specialist. Remember from our earlier discussions that those who put together evaluations or surveys are likely to fall into the brainstorming trap and list as much as possible rather than settling for a few particular points. The problem is that few people are able to excel at fifteen different qualities. If a particular leader would score strongly in just one area, he might be rated "exceptional" by those employees who have a need for this particular leadership quality. But this is better than being rated "mediocre" in all fifteen areas. If you can specialize in one talent or quality you have a better chance of succeeding in leadership than if you are a "jack of all trades." Just as individual team member skills and methods differ and *should* differ, so do individual leadership skills and methods.

Another thing to keep in mind when evaluating your team leader is that people with similar personalities and outlooks on life may get along better with each other than those with different personalities and outlooks, and some employees may therefore give the team leader a higher rating than others. In this sense, the team leader evaluation can become subjective rather than objective or scientific. This does not in itself mean that one person's evaluation is more correct than another's; it only means that a particular leader is a better "pitcher" for you than for somebody else. This is yet a reason why you should give specific examples when answering the questions on the evaluation and avoid simple "yes" or "no" answers, or worse, give the team leader a three on a scale of five. Keep in mind that under different circumstances, in a different company, with a different mission, or with a different team, the score might have been different, too.

Finally, for a team leader/supervisor evaluation to have meaning, the team leader must listen to what the employees are really saying on the evaluation. Written surveys with specific questions and multiple choice answers ranging from dislike to like are not accurate, because these sorts of answers are void of meaning and therefore difficult to compile into something meaningful. Answers need to be qualified with explanations or definitions if we are to ensure that everybody really understands what is being said. As an alternative, the team leader might want to listen in causally to what is being said in the break room and behind the scenes to get an idea of how the employees really think and feel. This approach will take a bit more work or dedication than simply handing out a survey, but it can be used as a tool for avoiding the application of a generic approach that will apply to nobody in particular when trying to fix problems. Remember that a great part of the leader's success has to do with how the team perceives him or her.

CAN YOU HEAR THE TALK?

No leadership book would be complete without mentioning the importance of proper communication. The ability to draw from the resourcefulness of your team can help you catch mistakes before they become morale destroyers. Good resource management emphasizes communication and the spread of information.

The person transmitting the message must demonstrate that he believes in the message he is sending. Great leaders have charisma that gives them the power to manipulate people's emotions. As Adolf Hitler said, "I know that fewer people are won over by the written word than by the spoken word, and that every great movement on this earth owes its growth to great speakers and not to great writers."[147] I am not asking that you approve of Adolf Hitler, but rather that you recognize that there is some truth to this statement. Great leaders can make you see logic where there is no truth. Great leaders can control the masses, but they can also abuse their power. Thus the receiver carries part of the responsibility for deciphering the message. A team leader that I know held a twenty-minute briefing, which was actually a twenty-minute one-man show. The dynamics of his delivery left no doubt in my mind that he believed strongly in the message and, after the lecture, I wanted to applaud him. But as I allowed the experience to settle, I discovered that what had kept me so captivated was not the message, but his *conviction*. In the end, there were few things he had said that I actually agreed with.

Although the leader must be passionate and committed to his cause if he is to inspire others to follow, a speech alone, although it might demonstrate passion, does not necessarily demonstrate commitment. Equally important, even if the leader is passionate and committed, he does not necessarily know the steps required to reach the goal or vision. Simply saying that you are committed to running the greatest business in the world will not allow you to accomplish this goal if you cannot also list the required steps and follow through on your commitment.

Communication is an active process that requires participation. Communication involves listening and understanding the other person's perceptions, which requires interaction between the speaker and the listener. Active listeners ask questions rather than finding something to argue about; they paraphrase the information to increase their understanding of what is being said. Passive listeners have already decided beforehand what they want to hear and can therefore not listen to what is really being said.

Leaders should ask questions to draw information from the employees. But questions intended to test an employee's knowledge, although valuable in certain other situations, have no place in communication. Effective questions are formed by asking what, where, how, and why. Listen with the intent of exploring the answer. To avoid confusion, make questions concise and ask only one thing at a time. Be sensible but also require that others give you a chance. When communicating, avoid questions that:

1. Are open-ended: "Do you have any questions?" The answer to an open-ended question is not likely to give you much new insight. It is simply too easy for the employee to say "no."

2. Are complex, require the person to solve a puzzle, or have a catch. This is not a test of who is smarter. The purpose of asking questions is not to quiz the employee on his or her knowledge, but to gain information. Moreover, employees are not mind readers. Contribute with information when you sense that an employee does not know where you are headed.

3. Cover everything: "What would you do to increase customer service?" It is better to ask a question that pertains to a particular situation: "When Mrs. Smith complained about the extra fee, name one thing you think we could have done that would have alleviated customer aggravation."

4. Give you a choice of this or that: "Should you greet the customer by first name or last name?" These questions are invalid because they force the person to make a choice even if both options are incorrect (or correct for that matter). Perhaps the customer prefers anonymity and does not want to be greeted by name at all.

5. Lead the employee to always answer "yes." For example: "Do you want a career that rewards you for your achievements?" Or, "Do you want to make six figures a year?" Well, duh, who wouldn't? Employees, beware! These types of questions usually have a hidden agenda. Think pyramid scheme. How much you earn in these types of jobs depends strictly on commission or how many incredibly long hours you work for peanuts. These sorts of jobs will make all but a tiny minority of top performers work themselves into the ground and lose everything, their money as well as their dignity. How do you guard against this type of manipulative behavior? You do a *Jack and Jill*, of course! Ask: What type of career? What types of rewards are we talking about? How are they distributed and in what amount? What kind of achievement does it take to earn a reward?

Answering questions posed by your team may seem easy particularly if you know the answer, but there is an art here as well:

1. Make sure you fully understand what is being asked and avoid mechanical answers. If in doubt, answer the question by asking another question along the same lines. This may lead the employee to answer his own question.

2. Look for a response when you have answered the question. If the employee seems confused, quiet, or indifferent, you might need to elaborate on your answer.

3. When an employee confronts you with a problem, ask a question that starts with "why" to trigger his thinking process. He may now find the solution himself. When we derive a solution through our own thinking, we will remember it better and give it greater approval.

4. Avoid yes or no answers. By giving a more thorough answer, you ensure that you really answer what is being asked.

5. It has been said that there are no dumb questions . . . only dumb people. Well, there are in fact both dumb questions and

dumb people. But when somebody asks a dumb question, do not ridicule him or tell him it is a "no-brainer." The purpose is to gain information and not to test an employee's intelligence. If you sense that an employee is afraid to ask but burns with a desire to know, be generous and take the first step by suggesting an answer or solution to a perceived problem.

Asking and answering questions also requires that you listen to what your team is really saying. Do you listen to everybody on your team, or do you listen more to the people you particularly like; to those who squeal the loudest; or to those who make an effort to seek you out? Do you ask your employees to clarify questions that you do not understand fully? If you do not know the correct answer, do you make an effort to find it? Do you let others finish speaking without interrupting, or do you "put words in their mouth?" If somebody is upset, they might just have a need to vent and not a need to argue. Are you honest and able to present and accept the facts, or do you push others to accept your values? Give an example. Do you know where you stand? Do you make your actions match your words? Sending mixed messages is detrimental to effective communication. Do you say a definite yes or no when you mean to say a definite yes or no? Do you think about what you want to say before you say it, so that you can say exactly what you want to say?

Furthermore, when conveying a new idea to your team, their attitudes may indicate resistance, passivity, or an unwillingness to comply. Barriers to communication include:

1. Lack of common background experiences. Understanding the team's background helps you determine the approach you should take when communicating.

2. Lack of commitment or lack of trust. How the transmitter and the receiver of the message feel during the exchange has an impact on how the message is perceived.

3. Physical and mental discomfort. When either the transmitter or the receiver is grouchy, ill, or uncomfortable, the

message may not be transmitted or received as intended, or may not be received at all. Remember my friend who once told me, "If it ain't right at home, it ain't right at work either"?

4. Argumentation. Recognize an invitation to argue and avoid it. Consider how your team will view you if you accept an argument openly. Note that argumentation is not synonymous with debate or discussion.

Now that you know how to ask and answer questions, can you hear the talk? Conflicts are not necessarily bad but become so when you fail to understand the essential issue. When a conflict is handled properly it will increase your confidence and deepen your thinking. Most managers say they have an "open door policy," yet many employees do not feel they can take advantage of it, because whenever they come with an issue to discuss it is immediately shot down. They are even interrupted when presenting it because the manager has already made up his mind. So, in fact, having an open door policy does not automatically make the manager more "approachable" even if he is "available." If people are uncomfortable talking with you it will not matter how "open" your door is, they will stop coming to you with suggestions or ideas; they will stop asking for your help; they will bypass you on the chain of command when something needs to get done. If you listen an awful lot but never take what is said to heart, people will begin to see the futility of the situation and stop wasting their time on you.

All sources of information are valuable, but few are as valuable as the person who uses his knowledge to guide others. Do not accept a challenge to prove a point. Keep sensitive issues behind closed doors and remember that people are people first before they are agents, workers, or employees. When times are bad it is fruitless to remind your team that they should be happy they have a job at all. People have emotions and when they are upset, they are not likely to respond to what you have to say. People do not listen or change when they are threatened or forced to do so. You must invite them in and meet them halfway. The transmitter must be ready, willing, and able to communicate the message. The receiver must be ready, willing, and able to receive the message. If we are concerned only with ourselves, we will say only what we want to say and hear only what we want to hear. Whether or not the wheel that squeaks gets the grease or silence is golden is a matter of timing. Whether or not a quiet person is a good or bad communicator is a matter of timing. The wheel turns one way, but it also turns the other way. Time a message right by asking, "Which way is the wheel turning?"

Now that you know something about communication, the final test is your ability to communicate the whole truth. If an employee asks about his future with the company and you give him a vague answer like, "There are opportunities for growth and development," what has he or she learned? Absolutely nothing! When the truth is spoken, it challenges people to get involved and creates commitment and team spirit. Withholding the truth creates insecurity. Lack of truthful communication challenges the workers to find the information through their own reasoning—through rumors. Rumors, faulty information, and worry steal energy from the workforce. Thus when you share information or discuss new policies with your people, state the truth, all of it. If you withhold certain facts you will be perceived as unreliable and dishonest. Bad news when told with sincerity and clear-sightedness will be taken in stride by the workers. It has been said that if you try to sit on two chairs at the same time, you will most likely fall in-between. Know on which chair you sit and face the truth with courage and honor. It is your responsibility as a leader to see and communicate things the way they are, and not the way you wish them to be.

A final warning: When communicating, do not put the buggy before the horse. When my shooting instructor was teaching me about the handgun he had me dry-fire it a few times. Then he loaded the gun, handed it to me, and said, "If you pull the trigger now, the gun will fire." My finger tightened on the trigger and I broke out in a cold sweat when I realized how close I had come to firing the gun inside my home. *Pull now!* was all I had heard because these were the action words. If he had put the horse before the buggy instead of the other way around he would have said, "Put the gun down, it is loaded," and then said, "If you were to pull the trigger now that the gun is loaded, the gun would fire."

So are the best leaders born or made? I don't know. I will let you decide.

CONCLUSION

Now that you have come to the end of this brief study about the critique of popular leadership approaches, whether you are a team leader or an employee you should know how to call things by their proper names and avoid hiding behind popular slogans and euphemism. You should know what it takes to be honest and clear-sighted when interacting with those around you, and how to recognize leadership ambiguities that can sabotage your best intentions and ruin your team. A leader will truly become a good leader only when he or she reflects on his experiences and analyzes why a particular approach did or did not work. However, simply reading a book is not likely to be of much help. There are literally hundreds of motivational leadership studies on the market, and most promise to reveal a new and innovative approach to leadership. Yet many of these books cast very little fresh light on the problems the leader faces every day. I believe it is safe to say that many of us read these books not because we are seeking something concrete that will inform us of how to behave, or that will contradict our previous views and therefore trigger some critical thinking, but because we want confirmation of the views that we already hold. The successful leader examines to what extent the information in these books is truthful and, if applied, whether it will help or hinder his or her particular situation. History does NOT repeat itself. Jeffrey Cohn, leadership advisor to chief executives, reminds us that one reason why we are bad at picking good leaders is because, "[a]t best, a 'track record' only tells half of the story. In a new position, the candidate will have to face new obstacles, deal with a new team, manage more people, introduce new products, and do it all without a clear roadmap."[148]

The question to ask is not how you want the employees to act or what you want them to accomplish, but *why*. Proper understanding brings depth of insight. The successful leader thus comments and questions and speaks of what he knows from experience and gut feeling. The successful leader moves forward with clarity of vision and sets some basic requirements for human intelligence. The successful leader seeks support from a team that is extraordinarily able and committed; he does a *Jack and Jill* (a dissection of the meaning) on every problem and asks as many questions pertaining to the scenario as possible. The successful leader acknowledges that being politically correct often blurs one's vision and challenges himself to see things as they are and do what is right. Practicing leadership means more than wearing the "supervisor" patch. You must actively seek out opportunities that help you improve your leadership skills. Furthermore, what one acquires is often a result of what one is searching for. Or as military historian Jay Luvaas put it: "A book is like a mirror. If an ass looks in, no prophet can peer out."[149]

The readers of leadership books would thus be wise to approach their studies with the same caution as a historian approaches his or her sources of information. You start by asking who wrote the book, what is his or her background, and what are the potential biases hidden within the text. What conviction does the author hold and what is he or she trying to achieve? Who is the primary beneficiary of the book? *Who Moved My Cheese? An Amazing Way to Deal with Change in Your Work and in Your Life* by Spencer Johnson and Kenneth Blanchard, for example, is clearly written to benefit the company and not the employee, despite the fact that it is often presented to employees and the parable of the two mice describes the actions the employees are expected to take when hard times strike. Simultaneously one should recognize that leadership studies can also be over-analyzed and result in a loss of direction.

The boundaries of leadership are ambiguous and cannot be authoritatively defined. This book has demonstrated that successful leadership requires disciplined and serious study rather than the popular "Believe It – Achieve It" type approach. Successful leadership is not a hard science like physics or mathematics but requires a great deal of individual judgment. Whether we like it or not, and as reinforced by a myriad of successful military leaders, leadership is not about expressing some particular "laws," but is more about bringing people into lockstep. Or as Adolf Hitler said, "The art of leadership, as displayed by really great popular leaders in all ages, consists in consolidating the attention of the people against a single adversary and taking care that nothing will split up that attention into sections."[150] Lastly this book has demonstrated that it is possible to arm yourself against the misuse, unintentional or otherwise, of a long row of popular leadership slogans and studies currently on the market.

Throughout the text I have cited a number of writers and Great Men to support my arguments or illustrate a point. Now might be a good time to revisit the quotes at the beginning of Parts I, II, and III, do a *Jack and Jill*, and ask how these might or might not apply to your particular leadership situation. As you do so, ask what the times and circumstances were when the statements were first uttered. If they were cherry-picked from a greater account, to what extent are they still true? You might want to start with the Adolf Hitler quote in the previous paragraph. Does it have continuity? Is leadership always or necessarily about "consolidating the attention of the people against a single adversary"? If you were to apply this statement to your leadership style, how would you do it? Give an example. Does history repeat itself? Why, or why not? Hitler also said, "A leader who has to abandon the platform founded on his general principles, because he recognizes the foundation as false, can act with honour only when he declares his readiness to accept the final consequences of his erroneous views."[151] Is there continuity between these statements, or is there a contradiction? Or is it more proper not to discuss Hitler at all and always regard his advice as false because of his lack of moral character?

You might also want to revisit some of the statements I made throughout the text and evaluate to what extent they are true. For example, how true is my claim that science is fascinating not because of the discoveries but because of the predictability; finding that the truth is in fact logic and steadfast, and that the concepts that were true a thousand years ago and earlier are still true today and most likely will be true tomorrow? Is science necessarily logic and steadfast? Has there ever been a time when we have proven a scientific principle false, perhaps many hundred years after its discovery? I also stated that for optimum team cohesion, people who like each other and want to work together should be placed together. Contrary to this view, some researchers state that there is no persuasive evidence that social cohesion is necessary to increase a group's effectiveness, and that people who don't like one another can still work well together.[152]

It should be clear by now that the common way of studying leadership may be "hostile" to leadership. To make the study of leadership a deep and intellectual undertaking and build a base for further exploration, we need to consider a multitude of sources and avoid focusing only on the type of leadership that is popular in the motivational book market. A good way to remain objective and avoid getting carried away by your passions, is by restating the opposition's viewpoint from *their* perspective as a check and balance on your own view. Or perhaps even add a third point of view: How would a bystander, either somebody totally unrelated to the situation or a customer, view the issue if he or she were allowed to observe and offer an opinion?

In a perfect world the study of leadership, similarly to the study of history as suggested by Swiss historian Jacob Burckhardt (1818-1897 CE), should not "make us clever for the next time, but make us wise forever."[153] Historians, as should leaders, deal with what has happened in the past but avoid making predictions or prescribing future behavior. A good historian does not push an ideology. Rather, he or she forms a thesis and examines the issues, and so should the leader. If the evidence reveals that the initial thesis will not work, the historian, as does the leader, changes the thesis rather than cherry-picks for evidence that supports the initial idea. Now, then, that you are armed with knowledge, move forward and educate the masses and arm them, too, with the thinking power they need to avoid stumbling into the wrong trench and getting conned by the long row of popular motivational leadership slogans and sayings. You will not always get it precisely right; however, you should also not be too far wrong. After all, leadership ain't rocket science!

NOTES

[1]See Niccolo Machiavelli, *The Art of War*, Constitution Society, http://www.constitution.org/mac/artofwar.txt.

[2]See Ralph Sawyer and Mei-chün Sawyer, *The Seven Military Classics of Ancient China* including the *Art of War* (Boulder, CO: Westview Press, 1993), 139.

[3]See General Tao Hanzhang, *Sun Tzu's Art of War: The Modern Chinese Interpretation*, translated by Yuan Shibing (New York, NY: Sterling Innovation, 2007), 69.

[4]Adrian Gostick and Chester Elton, *The Carrot Principle: How the Best Managers Use Recognition to Engage Their Employees, Retain Talent, and Drive Performance* (New York, NY: Free Press, 2007), 28.

[5]See Michael Pillsbury, *China Debates the Future Security Environment* (Washington D.C.: National Defense University Press, 2000), xxiii.

[6]Adolf Hitler, *Mein Kampf* (Boring, OR: CPA Book Publisher, first published in 1939), 38. Hitler also said, "Generally speaking, one should guard against considering the broad masses more stupid than they really are." Ibid., 105. Which of these two statements from *Mein Kampf* is correct? Which one would you use to support the views you hold? Hopefully you will see how easy it is to cherry-pick sentences as one sees fit from any larger account and find the idea or slogan one needs in support of one's views. The Bible might be the book that has been cherry-picked more than any other.

[7]Ibid., 43. To be fair it should be pointed out that there were German men and women who did not fall in lockstep with Hitler's ideals. A few voiced their opposition openly, but many more neither supported nor opposed the coming tragedy. However, as evidenced by numerous film clips and other documentation, the broad masses screamed with joy when Joseph Goebbels held his famous speech about total war in 1943.

[8]Edward Whymper, *Scrambles Amongst the Alps in the Years 1860-69* (Philadelphia, PA: J. B. Lippincott & Co., 1872), 162.

[9]Marcus Buckingham and Curt Coffman, *First, Break All the Rules: What the World's Greatest Managers Do Differently* (New York, NY: Simon & Schuster, 1999), 53.

[10]Robert D. Kaplan, "On Forgetting the Obvious," *The American Interest Online* (Jul.-Aug. 2007), http://www.the-american-interest.com/article.cfm?piece=289.

[11]See Sawyer, 162.

[12]Ibid., 161.

[13]Richard Marcinko, *Leadership Secrets of the Rogue Warrior: A Commando's Guide to Success* (New York, NY: Pocket Books, 1996), 129.

[14]Ibid., 155.

[15]See Zhuge Liang, *The Way of the General*, translated by Thomas Cleary, http://kongming.net/novel/writings/wotg/2.php.

[16]See Jennifer Robison, "Lt. General Russel L. Honoré: A Military General's Leadership Lessons," *Gallup Management Journal* (Jan. 8, 2009).

[17]Ibid.

[18]Ibid.

[19]See Owen Connelly, *On War and Leadership: The Words of Combat Commanders from Frederick the Great to Norman Schwarzkopf* (Princeton, NJ: Princeton University Press, 2002), 12.

[20]Ibid.

[21]Donald T. Phillips, *Lincoln on Leadership: Executive Strategies for Tough Times* (New York, NY: Warner Books, 1992), 13.

[22]See H. W. Crocker III, *Robert E. Lee on Leadership: Executive Lessons in Character, Courage, and Vision* (New York, NY: Three Rivers Press, 2004), Kindle Edition.

[23]See Marcinko, *Leadership Secrets of the Rogue Warrior*, 72.

[24]Ibid., 108.

[25]See Richard Marcinko, *The Rogue Warrior's Strategy for Success: A Commando's Principles of Winning* (New York, NY: Pocket Books, 1997), 13.

[26]Ibid., 94.

[27]Chuck Yeager, Famous Quotes, http://www.icelebz.com/quotes/chuck_yeager/.

[28]Richard Hiner, "Instructor Report," *Air Safety Foundation* (First Quarter, 2005).

[29]Snorri Sturluson, *King Olaf Trygvason's Saga*, Internet Sacret Text Archive, http://www.sacred-texts.com/neu/heim/07olaftr.htm.

[30]See Nassir Ghaemi, *A First-Rate Madness: Uncovering the Links Between Leadership and Mental Illness* (New York, NY: Penguin Press, 2011), Kindle Edition.

[31]See Marcinko, *Leadership Secrets of the Rogue Warrior,* 6.

[32]Ghaemi.

[33]Thucydides, *The Peloponnesian War: The Complete Hobbes Translation* with notes and introduction by David Grene (Chicago, IL: University of Chicago Press, 1989), 1-2.

[34]Ibid., 3.

[35]Ibid., 32.

[36]Ibid., 50.

[37]Ibid., 67.

[38]Ibid., 46.

[39]Ibid., 67-68.

[41]See Thucydides, *The History of the Peloponnesian War*, Kindle Edition.

[41]Ibid.

[42]Xenophon, *The March Up Country: A Translation of Xenophon's Anabasis*, translated by W. H. D. Rouse (Ann Arbor: MI: University of Michigan Press, 2001), 91.

[43]Ibid., 99.

[44]Ibid., 96-97.

[45]Ibid., 95.

[46]Ibid., 98.

[47]Ibid., 90.

[48]Ibid., 89.

[49]Ibid., 109.

[50]See Julius Caius Caesar, *De Bello Gallico & Other Commentaries of Caius Julius Caesar*, translated by W. A. Macdevitt (1929), 9.

[51]Ibid., 4.

[52]Ibid., 5.

[53]Ibid., 2.

[54]Ibid., 2.

[55]Ibid., 6.

[56]Ibid., 12.

[57]Ibid., 26.

[58]Ibid., 6.

[59]Ibid., 20.

[60]Ibid., 3.

[61]Ibid., 15.

[62]Ibid., 15.

[63]Johann von Ewald, *Diary of the American War: A Hessian Journal*, translated and edited by Joseph P. Tustin (New Haven, CT: Yale University Press, 1979), 21.

[64]Ibid., 18.

[65]Ibid., 25.

[66]Ibid., 19.

[67]Ibid., 42.

[68]Ibid., 42.

[69]Ibid., 45.

[70]Ibid., 354.

[71]Ibid., 44.

[72]Ibid., 355.

[73]Ibid., 354.

[74]Ibid., 355.

[75]Ibid., 356.

[76]Ibid., 361.

[77]Ibid., 34.

[78]See Armand de Caulaincourt, *With Napoleon in Russia: The Memoirs of General de Caulaincourt, Duke of Vicenza* (New York, NY: William Morrow, 1935), 48.

[79]Ibid., 63.

[80]Ibid., 87.

[81]Ibid., 103.

[82]Ibid., 52.

[83]Ibid., 60.

[84]Ibid., 61.

[85]Ibid., 46.

[86]Ibid., 49.

[87]Ibid., 64.

[88]Ibid., 67.

[89]Ibid., 70.

[90]Ibid., 72.

[91]See Russell F. Weigley, *The American Way of War: A History of United States Military Strategy and Policy* (Bloomington, IN: Indiana University Press, 1973), 215.

[92]See Carl von Clausewitz, *On War*, edited and translated by Michael Howard and Peter Paret (Princeton, NJ: Princeton University Press, 1976), 193.

[93]See John Shy, *Makers of Modern Strategy: From Machiavelli to the Nuclear Age*, edited by Peter Paret (Princeton, NJ: Princeton University Press, 1986), 167.

[94]Antoine-Henri Jomini, *The Art of War*, translated by H. Mendell and W. P. Craighill (Philadelphia, PA: Lippincott, 1879), Article VIII.

[95]Ibid., Article XIV.

[96]Shy, 173.

[97]Ibid., 174.

[98]Carl von Clausewitz, *On War: A Modern Military Classic* (Radford, VA: Wilder Publications, 2008), 133.

[99]See Allan R. Millett and Peter Maslowski, *For the Common Defense: A Military History of the United States of America* (New York, NY: The Free Press, 1994), 172-173.

[100]From H. P. Willmott lecture about *Jomini and The Art of War*, Norwich University, VT, 2006.

[101]See Ian Morris, *Why the West Rules—For Now* (New York, NY: Farrar, Straus and Giroux, 2010), 27,

[102]See Sawyer, 51.

[103]See Quotes Papa, *16 Xenophon Quotes and Sayings*, http://www.quotespapa.com/authors/xenophon-quotes.html.

[104]Kaplan.

[105]Heraclitus, Wikiquote, http://en.wikiquote.org/wiki/Heraclitus.

[106]See PBS, "The Persuaders," *Frontline*, http://www.pbs.org/wgbh/pages/frontline/shows/persuaders/view/.

[107]See Dallas D. Irvine, "The French Discovery of Clausewitz and Napoleon," *The Journal of the American Military Institute*, Vol. 4, No. 3 (Autumn 1940), 144.

[108]See Hew Strachan, *Clausewitz's On War* (New York, NY: Atlantic Monthly Press, 2007), 97.

[109]Ibid., 98-99.

[110]See Marcinko, *Leadership Secrets of the Rogue Warrior*, frontmatter.

[111]Niccolo Machiavelli, *The Historical, Political, and Diplomatic Writings of Niccolo Machiavelli*, Vol. 2, translated by Christian E. Detmold (Boston, MA: James R. Osgood and Company, 1882), 422.

[112]See Michael C. C. Adams, *The Best War Ever: America and World War II* (Baltimore, MD: The John Hopkins University Press, 1994), 5.

[113]Aaron David Miller, *The Much Too Promised Land: America's Elusive Search for Arab-Israeli Peace* (New York, NY: Bantam Dell, 2008), 127.

[114]See Stephen C. Lundin, et al., *Fish! A Remarkable Way to Boost Morale and Improve Results* (New York, NY: Hyperion, 2000), 15-18 & 57.

[115]See Spencer Johnson and Kenneth Blanchard, *Who Moved My Cheese? An Amazing Way to Deal with Change in Your Work and in Your Life* (New York, NY: Putnam & Sons, 1998), 21.

[116]See Barbara Ehrenreich, *Bright-Sided: How the Relentless Promotion of Positive Thinking Has Undermined America* (New York, NY: Metropolitan Books, 2009), 9.

[117]Ibid., 115.

[118]Ibid., 199.

[119]Buckingham and Coffman, 141.

[120]See Wystan Hugh Auden, Wikiquote, http://en.wikiquote.org/wiki/W._H._Auden.

[121]Buckingham and Coffman, 133-134.

[122]Gostick and Elton, 27 & 58.

[123]Ibid., 9.

[124]See John C. Maxwell, *The 21 Indispensible Qualities of a Leader: Becoming the Person Others Will Want to Follow* (Nashville, TN: Thomas Nelson, 2007), 4.

[125]Daniel H. Pink, "Big Bonuses Don't Mean Big Results," *Special to CNN* (Mar. 2, 2010).

[126]See Gostick and Elton, 87.

[127]Joseph Heller, *Catch-22* (New York, NY: Alfred A. Knopf, 2011), 56.

[128]The author is indebted to Professor Art Ritter at Westminster College in Salt Lake City for teaching how and why to ask the appropriate questions.

[129]Friedrich Nietzsche, Wikipedia, http://en.wikipedia.org/wiki/Friedrich_Nietzsche.

[130]Sigmund Freud, "Sigmund Freud Quotes," *Notable Quotes,* http://www.notable-quotes.com/f/freud_sigmund.html. There is some controversy as to whether or not this statement should actually be attributed to Sigmund Freud.

[131]Ed Parker, *Infinite Insights Into Kenpo: Mental Stimulation* (Los Angeles, CA: Delsby Publications,1982), 58.

[132]See Kitty Campbell, "Influence Employees the Right Way," *All Business* (May 1, 2002), http://www.allbusiness.com/human-resources/workforce-management/209349-1.html.

[133]See Franklin D. Scott, *Sweden: The Nation's History* (Carbondale, IL: Southern Illinois University Press, 1988), 65.

[134]Aristotle, Dictionary.com, Quotation by Aristotle, quotes.dictionary.com.

[135]Ehrenreich, 198.

[136]See Clausewitz, *On War*, 584.

[137]The author challenges the reader to consider to what extent this statement is true. Is science necessarily logic and steadfast? Has there ever been a time when we have proven a scientific principle false, perhaps many hundred years after its discovery?

[138]See Francis Bacon, Wikiquote, http://en.wikiquote.org/wiki/Knowledge.

[139]Ghaemi.

[140]Buckingham and Coffman, 172- 173.

[141]Ibid., 61-62.

[142]Ibid., 173.

[143]Ibid., 256.

[144]Supposedly said by Petronius Arbiter in the days of ancient Rome; although, it is disputed if he actually said this. See Richard A. Clarke, *Your Government Failed You: Breaking the Cycle of National Security Disasters* (New York, NY: HarperCollins Publishers, 2008), 205.

[145]See Paul G. Hewitt, *Conceptual Physics* (Glenview, IL: Scott, Foresman and Company, 1989), or any other book on elementary physics for further definition and information about the terms used here.

[146]Campbell.

[147]Hitler, 6.

[148]Jeffrey Cohn, "Why We Pick Bad Leaders, and How to Spot the Good Ones," *Special to CNN* (Feb. 14, 2012), http://www.cnn.com/2012/02/14/opinion/cohn-pick-leaders/index.html?hpt=hp_c3.

[149]Jay Luvaas, "Military History: Is It Still Practicable?" *Parameters* (Mar. 1982).

[150]Hitler, 75.

[151]Ibid., 47. It might be interesting to observe how Hitler noted the difficulty of finding people who are simultaneously great theorists and great leaders. To be a leader, he said, "means to be able to move the masses." But merely formulating ideas as theorists do, "has nothing whatsoever to do with the capacity for leadership." Yet to move the masses we need intellectual theorists for support. With respect to Great Men who have shaped the course of history he defined them as follows: "The noblest conception of the human understanding remain without purpose or value if the leader cannot move the masses towards them, and, conversely, what would it avail to have all the genius and *élan* of a leader if the intellectual theorist does not fix the aims for which mankind must struggle. But when the abilities of theorist and organizer and leader are united in the one person, then we have the rarest phenomenon on this earth, and it is that union which produces the great man." Hitler, 319.

[152]See Leonard Wong, et al., "Why They Fight: Combat Motivation in the Iraq War," *Strategic Studies Institute* (July 2003), 4-5.

[153]Jacob Burckhardt, *Quotations on History*, compiled by Robert Blackey, http://history.csusb.edu/facultyStaff/History306/HistoryQuotations 8_16_96.pdf.

BIBLIOGRAPHY

Adams, Michael C. C. *The Best War Ever: America and World War II.* Baltimore, MD: The John Hopkins University Press, 1994.

Aristotle. Dictionary.com. Quotation by Aristotle. Quotes.dictionary.com.

Auden, Wystan Hugh. Wikiquote. http://en.wikiquote.org/wiki/W._H._Auden.

Bacon, Francis. Wikiquote. http://en.wikiquote.org/wiki/Knowledge.

Buckingham, Marcus and Coffman, Curt. *First, Break All the Rules: What the World's Greatest Managers Do Differently.* New York, NY: Simon & Schuster, 1999.

Burckhardt, Jacob. *Quotations on History.* Compiled by Robert Blackey. http://history.csusb.edu/facultyStaff/History306/HistoryQu otations8_16_96.pdf.

Caesar, Julius Caius. *De Bello Gallico & Other Commentaries of Caius Julius Caesar.* Translated by W. A. Macdevitt (1929).

Campbell, Kitty. "Influence Employees the Right Way." *All Business* (May 1, 2002). http://www.allbusiness.com/human-resources/workforce-management/209349-1.html.

Caulaincourt, Armand de. *With Napoleon in Russia: The Memoirs of General de Caulaincourt, Duke of Vicenza.* New York, NY: William Morrow, 1935.

Clarke, Richard A. *Your Government Failed You: Breaking the Cycle of National Security Disasters.* New York, NY: HarperCollins Publishers, 2008.

Clausewitz, Carl von. *On War: A Modern Military Classic.* Radford, VA: Wilder Publications, 2008.

.........*On War.* Edited and translated by Michael Howard and Peter Paret. Princeton, NJ: Princeton University Press, 1976.

Cohn, Jeffrey. "Why We Pick Bad Leaders, and How to Spot the Good Ones." *Special to CNN* (Feb. 14, 2012). http://www.cnn.com/2012/02/14/opinion/cohn-pick-leaders/index.html?hpt=hp_c3.

Connelly, Owen. *On War and Leadership: The Words of Combat Commanders from Frederick the Great to Norman Schwarzkopf.* Princeton, NJ: Princeton University Press, 2002.

Crocker, H. W., III. *Robert E. Lee on Leadership: Executive Lessons in Character, Courage, and Vision.* New York, NY: Three Rivers Press, 2004.

Ehrenreich, Barbara. *Bright-Sided: How the Relentless Promotion of Positive Thinking Has Undermined America.* New York, NY: Metropolitan Books, 2009.

Ewald, Johann von. *Diary of the American War: A Hessian Journal.* Translated and edited by Joseph P. Tustin. New Haven, CT: Yale University Press, 1979.

Freud, Sigmund. "Sigmund Freud Quotes." *Notable Quotes.* http://www.notable-quotes.com/f/freud_sigmund.html.

Ghaemi, Nassir. *A First-Rate Madness: Uncovering the Links Between Leadership and Mental Illness*. New York, NY: Penguin Press, 2011.

Gostick, Adrian and Elton, Chester. *The Carrot Principle: How the Best Managers Use Recognition to Engage Their Employees, Retain Talent, and Drive Performance*. New York, NY: Free Press, 2007.

Heller, Joseph. *Catch-22*. New York, NY: Alfred A. Knopf, 2011.

Heraclitus. Wikiquote. http://en.wikiquote.org/wiki/Heraclitus.

Hewitt, Paul G. *Conceptual Physics*. Glenview, IL: Scott, Foresman and Company, 1989.

Hiner, Richard. "Instructor Report." *Air Safety Foundation* (First Quarter, 2005).

Hitler, Adolf. *Mein Kampf*. Boring, OR: CPA Book Publisher. First published in 1939.

Irvine, Dallas D. "The French Discovery of Clausewitz and Napoleon." *The Journal of the American Military Institute*, Vol. 4, No. 3 (Autumn 1940).

Johnson, Spencer and Blanchard, Kenneth. *Who Moved My Cheese? An Amazing Way to Deal with Change in Your Work and in Your Life*. New York, NY: Putnam & Sons, 1998.

Jomini, Antoine-Henri. *The Art of War*. Translated by H. Mendell and W. P. Craighill. Philadelphia, PA: Lippincott, 1879.

Kaplan, Robert D. "On Forgetting the Obvious." *The American Interest Online* (Jul.-Aug. 2007). http://www.the-american-interest.com/article.cfm?piece=289.

Lundin, Stephen C., et al. *Fish! A Remarkable Way to Boost Morale and Improve Results*. New York, NY: Hyperion, 2000.

Luvaas, Jay. "Military History: Is It Still Practicable?" *Parameters* (Mar. 1982).

Machiavelli, Niccolo. *The Art of War*. Constitution Society. http://www.constitution.org/mac/artofwar.txt.

.........*The Historical, Political, and Diplomatic Writings of Niccolo Machiavelli*, Vol. 2. Translated by Christian E. Detmold. Boston, MA: James R. Osgood and Company, 1882.

Marcinko, Richard. *Leadership Secrets of the Rogue Warrior: A Commando's Guide to Success*. New York, NY: Pocket Books, 1996.

.........*The Rogue Warrior's Strategy for Success: A Commando's Principles of Winning*. New York, NY: Pocket Books, 1997.

Maxwell, John C. *The 21 Indispensible Qualities of a Leader: Becoming the Person Others Will Want to Follow*. Nashville, TN: Thomas Nelson, 2007.

Miller, Aaron David. *The Much Too Promised Land: America's Elusive Search for Arab-Israeli Peace*. New York, NY: Bantam Dell, 2008.

Millet, Allan R. and Maslowski, Peter. *For the Common Defense: A Military History of the United States of America*. New York, NY: The Free Press, 1994.

Morris, Ian. *Why the West Rules—For Now*. New York, NY: Farrar, Straus and Giroux, 2010.

Nietzsche, Friedrich. Wikipedia. http://en.wikipedia.org/wiki/Friedrich_Nietzsche.

Parker, Ed. *Infinite Insights Into Kenpo: Mental Stimulation*. Los Angeles, CA: Delsby Publications, 1982.

PBS. "The Persuaders." *Frontline*. http://www.pbs.org/wgbh/pages/frontline/shows/persuaders /view/.

Phillips, Donald T. *Lincoln on Leadership: Executive Strategies for Tough Times*. New York, NY: Warner Books, 1992.

Pillsbury, Michael. *China Debates the Future Security Environment*. Washington D.C.: National Defense University Press, 2000.

Pink, Daniel H. "Big Bonuses Don't Mean Big Results." *Special to CNN* (Mar. 2, 2010).

Quotes Papa. *16 Xenophon Quotes and Sayings*. http://www.quotespapa.com/authors/xenophon-quotes.html.

Robison, Jennifer. "Lt. General Russel L. Honoré: A Military General's Leadership Lessons." *Gallup Management Journal* (Jan. 8, 2009).

Sawyer, Ralph and Sawyer, Mei-chün. *The Seven Military Classics of Ancient China* including the *Art of War*. Boulder, CO: Westview Press, 1993.

Scott, Franklin D. *Sweden: The Nation's History*. Carbondale, IL: Southern Illinois University Press, 1988.

Shy, John. *Makers of Modern Strategy: From Machiavelli to the Nuclear Age*. Edited by Peter Paret. Princeton, NJ: Princeton University Press, 1986.

Strachan, Hew. *Clausewitz's On War*. New York, NY: Atlantic Monthly Press, 2007.

Sturluson, Snorri. *King Olaf Trygvason's Saga*. Internet Sacret Text Archive. http://www.sacred-texts.com/neu/heim/07olaftr.htm.

Tao Hanzhang, General. *Sun Tzu's Art of War: The Modern Chinese Interpretation*. Translated by Yuan Shibing. New York, NY: Sterling Innovation, 2007.

Thucydides. *The History of the Peloponnesian War*. Kindle Edition.

.........*The Peloponnesian War: The Complete Hobbes Translation* with notes and introduction by David Grene. Chicago, IL: University of Chicago Press, 1989.

Weigley, Russell F. *The American Way of War: A History of United States Military Strategy and Policy*. Bloomington, IN: Indiana University Press, 1973.

Whymper, Edward. *Scrambles Amongst the Alps in the Years 1860-69*. Philadelphia, PA: J. B. Lippincott & Co., 1872.

Willmott, H. P. Lecture about *Jomini and The Art of War*. Norwich University, VT, 2006.

Wong, Leonard, et al. "Why They Fight: Combat Motivation in the Iraq War." *Strategic Studies Institute* (July 2003).

Xenophon. *The March Up Country: A Translation of Xenophon's Anabasis*. Translated by W. H. D. Rouse. Ann Arbor: MI: University of Michigan Press, 2001.

Yeager, Chuck. Famous Quotes. http://www.icelebz.com/quotes/chuck_yeager/.

Zhuge Liang. *The Way of the General*. Translated by Thomas Cleary. http://kongming.net/novel/writings/wotg/2.php.

About the Author

Martina Sprague has a Master of Arts Degree in Military History from Norwich University in Vermont. As a historian she is particularly interested in political and social factors that influence the decisions of "Great Men" and the actions of their subordinates. She has written numerous books about military and political/social history. For more information, please visit her Web site: www.modernfighter.com.